CLARKSON POTTER/
PUBLISHERS
New York

back pocket pasta

INSPIRED DINNERS TO COOK ON THE FLY

Colu Henry

Photographs by **PEDEN + MUNK**

Copyright © 2017 by Colu Henry
Photographs copyright © 2017 by
Peden + Munk

All rights reserved.
Published in the United States by
Clarkson Potter/Publishers, an imprint
of the Crown Publishing Group, a
division of Penguin Random House
LLC, New York.
crownpublishing.com
clarksonpotter.com

CLARKSON POTTER is a trademark
and POTTER with colophon is a
registered trademark of Penguin
Random House LLC.

Library of Congress Cataloging-in-
Publication Data is available upon
request.

ISBN 978-0-553-45974-6
eBook ISBN 978-0-553-45975-3

Printed in China

Cover design by Jennifer K. Beal Davis
Book design by Stephanie Huntwork
Cover and interior photographs by
Peden + Munk

10 9 8 7 6 5 4 3 2 1

First Edition

For my mama,
MIA FERRARA HENRY,
for telling me "I think I can."
I did.

contents

introduction

We all tend to get hung up on recipes, but long lists of ingredients and steps aren't actually that helpful for weeknight cooking. Everyone should be able to reach for what's closest and pull together something nourishing and beautiful without fuss. What's most beneficial is to set up your pantry, stock your fridge, and open your eyes to what works well together. Simple, high-quality ingredients allow you to cut your hardworking self a break and, most important, have fun while doing so.

When I worked in food publishing and public relations, one might have believed that all I did was eat out (I did, quite a bit), but the truth was, when I wasn't dining out, I was coming home weary from work (like most of us) and just wanted an easy dinner that I didn't have to shop for. Something soulful but simple that, with a bottle of wine, could take the rest of the day away.

I started pulling together dishes with the thing I know best—pasta—and using whatever items I had lying about. I would put the pot of water on to boil and in the meantime, rummage through my cupboards cobbling a dish together. I'd sauté garlic and red pepper flakes, melt anchovies into olive oil, toss in leftover greens to wilt, and chop and toast whatever nuts I had for a topping. Before I knew it, we were sitting down for dinner. Eager to share my creations with friends to help them get out of their own weeknight rut, I started posting photos online, tagging them #backpocketpasta. Post-work cooking suddenly went from daunting to delightful.

I am the great-granddaughter of Italian immigrants. Maria-Nicola—my namesake, who also went by the name Colu—and my great-grandfather Pietro emigrated from Italy. They hailed from a small village called Teora in the province of Avellino in southern Italy. Seventeen years old at the time of their crossing, they, like millions of other immigrants, arrived in this country with nothing. My nonni, Immacolata Ferrara—who went by Molly for short—was the eldest of their seven children (only five survived) and was born here in 1909. She lived until she was 102 and recounted in our discussions that with many mouths to feed, Colu's recipes were born out of poverty and necessity. She would cook with whatever ingredients she happened to have on hand, and with whatever was available at the market, but always took great care with her meals. Most of my great-grandmother's recipes were passed down verbally to my nonni and then from my nonni to my mother, Mia, and her brothers, Michael and John. As a child, I would listen to the stories that surrounded these recipes—tales that still excite me just as much as actually assembling the dishes themselves.

Growing up, we ate pasta two or three times a week. Marinara and tuna-clam sauce were in constant rotation, but Sundays were the best days. I would wake up to the smell of meatballs frying in olive oil and sauce simmering on the stove. Sometimes there was a lone pork chop that needed a home, and if we were extra lucky, we'd also have braciole with pine nuts and raisins to look forward to. Sleepily, I would throw off my covers and rush downstairs for a plate of sauce, a meatball, and lots of grated Pecorino Romano. If Mama had a semolina sesame loaf from Arthur Avenue on hand, even better. Breakfast was served.

Sunday's meat sauce is only one of many culinary traditions that we celebrated as a family. There was the Feast of the Seven Fishes on Christmas Eve (my personal favorite), minestra and *pizza rustica* on Easter Sunday, and countless others. And although my family has tweaked the recipes here and there over the years, we still use many of my great-grandmother's and nonni's scribbled notes to guide us in the kitchen.

These days my husband, Chad, and I split our time between Brooklyn and Hudson, New York, with our spaniel rescue mutt, Joshie, and we also travel as much as we can. The pastas I cook are always at the mercy of the pantries to which I have access. For instance, what I make Chad for dinner after a ten-hour workday is different from what I create when I'm visiting my mom for the weekend or what we prepare for a traditional holiday at my uncle Michael's. That said, all the recipes I've included in this book are inspired by the same principle. If you have a well-stocked pantry and shop somewhat seasonally, a back pocket pasta is never more than a pot of boiling water away.

here's how it works

Back Pocket Pasta is less a cookbook and more a loose guide and inspiration for making weeknight dinners artfully and on the fly. My hope is that this book will give you ideas and recipes on how to create your own back pocket pastas with just a few ingredients on hand. No two pantries are the same, so you should feel free to play around with ingredients. If you like extra heat, add more chiles. If you prefer broccoli rabe to Brussels sprouts, swap them out. Pancetta or prosciutto? You choose. Cooking is already more fun, isn't it?

PASTA DON'T PREACH

While I'm a pretty laid-back cook, there are a few things I *always* do:

1. **Salt the water well.** Well-seasoned water is key to pasta perfection, so I add about 2 tablespoons (or two small palmfuls) of kosher salt to every large stockpot of boiling water.

2. **Cook the pasta al dente.** I generally follow the rules of what's on the pasta box as they provide cooking times for pastas to maintain its to-the-bite texture (very important). I also often taste the pasta a minute or so before it's supposed to be done, just to ensure it's not overcooking. You don't want soggy pasta.

3. **Save the pasta water.** That salty, starchy liquid is my secret weapon for bringing together the sauce. Rather than draining the pasta in the sink, I pull it out with tongs or a pasta spider and throw it directly in the sauce, so the water can stay in the pot and you can add more in as needed.

4. **Have the sauce ready when the pasta is done.** Drained, dried-out pasta waiting for sauce to finish is *no bene*. I time everything so it finishes together.

5. **Toss the pasta in the sauce.** A great pasta dish happens in those last few minutes when everything comes together.

ALL BOXED UP

You'll notice that all of my recipes call for three-quarters of a pound of dried pasta (or three-quarters of a box of pasta). I prefer less pasta to more sauce, but you can absolutely cook the whole box of pasta and save a fourth of it for another night if you wish. Many dried pasta choices line the supermarket aisles, but I prefer the Barilla brand which is easy to find, and I think it has the best texture. Here are some tips on what you can do with those leftovers:

- Cooked pasta freezes well. Add it directly to simmered broth with fresh vegetables for a quick weeknight soup.

- Make a pasta frittata with leftover pasta, eggs, cheese, and whatever vegetables you have lying about in your fridge.

LET'S GET SAUCED

Almost every recipe in the book calls for "loosening up" the sauce with pasta water. What I mean by that is to use the pasta cooking water to slightly thin out your sauce. How much water you add is really up to you; my mama likes her sauce to have lots of liquid (great for sopping up with bread!) and she tends to add more than I do. Bottom line, you want all of the pasta to be amply covered and slick with the sauce so the sauce doesn't just sit on top of the pasta. Even coverage is key.

Tomato sauces generally won't need as much additional water as a "white" sauce, because tomatoes already have a lot of moisture. Start with ¼ cup of water and take it from there. Sometimes you'll need more, sometimes you won't. If you do happen to add too much pasta water, don't fret, just add grated Pecorino Romano or Parmesan and cook for a minute over medium-high heat to help bring everything back together. Cheese always makes everything better.

SET UP YOUR STATION

Before I start cooking anything, I'll have everything within arm's length. Putting out all the tools you need to cook with ahead of time helps you pull together an improvised pasta with ease. Here's what I always keep close at hand:

- Large stockpot and a 12-inch skillet

- Large cutting board and sharp knife

- Wooden spoon or spatula

- Pasta claw, spider skimmer, or tongs

- Ladle

- Microplane or cheese grater

I also keep my food processor on the countertop to help make quick work of pestos and other sauces, but that's totally up to you.

LET'S DRINK!

At the back of the book you'll find a few drink recipes from one of my dearest friends, Talia Baiocchi—editor in chief of *PUNCH,* an online magazine about cocktails, wine, and spirits—for some very cool *apertivis* to make while pulling together your own back pocket pasta, as well a short primer on wine pairings and navigating your local wine store. Because honestly what is a pasta dinner without *vino*? Nothing I tell you. Nothing!

   I'm excited for you to dive in and get started. I hope you'll enjoy reading and cooking from this book as much as I've enjoyed putting it together. *Buon appetito!*

PASTA SHAPES & SIZES

Different pasta shapes work better with certain sauces. Here's a quick go-to guide to help you choose.

LONG AND LEAN
Pastas like linguine, spaghetti, and linguine fini are best with non-tomato-based sauces that cling to the noodle without drowning it. Thicker long pasta like tagliatelle, fusilli lunghi, and fettuccine have the real estate to handle richer ragus and cream sauces.

TUBULAR

Pastas such as rigatoni, paccheri, and penne can stand up to heavier, chunkier sauces. Think sauces that incorporate beans and ones that are meat-driven. The middle of the pasta will capture bits of sauce, allowing you to construct the ultimate bite.

SHORT AND CURVY

Fusilli, gemelli, campanelle, and others are the most versatile—perfect for catching bits of vegetables, meat, and seafood in their nooks. They also work well with a simple marinara or just plain butter and cheese.

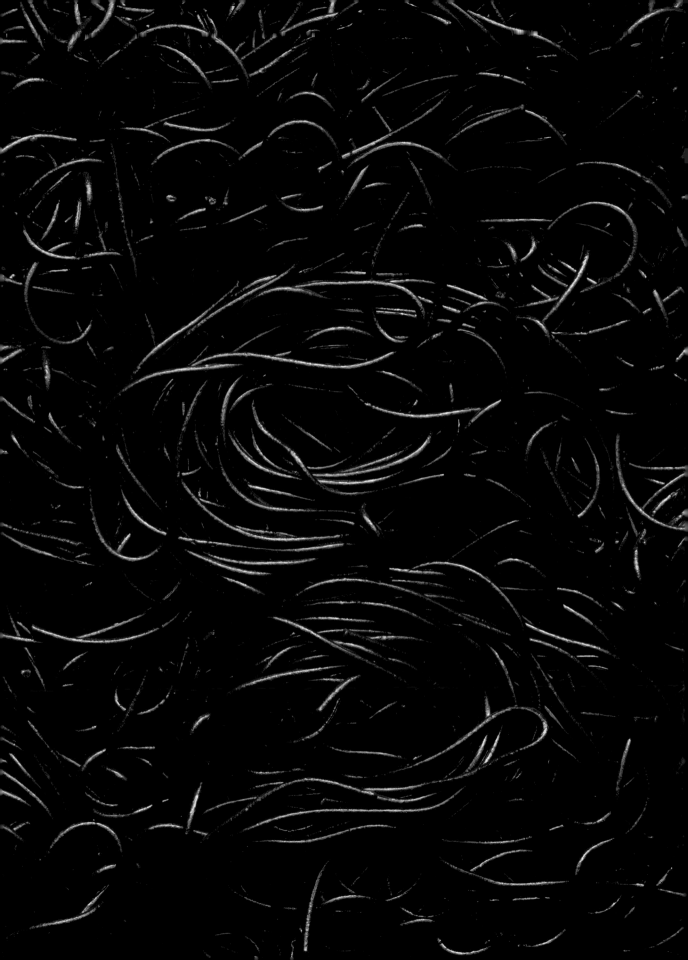

mama's

from Teora to the tenements

BUTTERY
BASIL PESTO
with LINGUINE

In the summer, my mama picks bushels of basil from her garden, which she turns into this creamy, vibrantly green pesto that I can never get enough of. Her trick is to make large quantities to freeze in ice cube trays, which she can later pop out and use throughout the winter. This recipe calls for plenty of butter and less oil than traditional recipes—and both Parmesan and Pecorino Romano. Try it and you'll see why it's in constant rotation at our house all year long.

SERVES 4

Kosher salt

¾ pound linguine fini or other long and thin pasta

2 cloves garlic

2 cups tightly packed basil leaves

2 tablespoons pine nuts

½ cup olive oil

½ cup grated Parmesan or Grana Padano

¼ cup grated Pecorino Romano cheese

4 tablespoons (½ stick) unsalted butter, at room temperature

Freshly ground black pepper (optional)

1. Bring a large pot of water to a boil. Add 2 tablespoons of the salt and return to a rolling boil. Add the pasta and cook until al dente according to package directions.

2. Meanwhile, in a food processor, combine the garlic, basil, pine nuts, oil, and a small pinch of salt and pulse until they form a bright green paste.

3. Transfer the mixture to a large bowl and fold in the Parmesan, Pecorino Romano, and butter. Season with additional salt and pepper, if desired.

4. Scoop the pasta directly into the bowl of pesto and toss together to coat, adding ¼ cup of pasta water or more (up to 1 cup), as needed to loosen up the sauce. Plate in warm bowls.

COOK'S NOTE: This pesto also acts as a lovely condiment. Spread it on thick sliced crusty bread and stuff with roasted vegetables or leftover cold roast chicken, or cut ripe tomatoes into fat wedges and drizzle some pesto on top and eat them with your hands.

TONNO & TOMATO with SWEET ONION

Tuna packed in good olive oil is a must for pasta dishes like this. If you can, wait to make this recipe with in-season tomatoes—when they're ripe enough that they slowly melt in the oil. I use Vidalia onion for its sweetness, but feel free to substitute what you have in your pantry: shallots, red onions, or stalwart yellow onions all work fine. **SERVES 4**

Kosher salt

3 tablespoons olive oil

½ medium Vidalia onion, halved and thinly sliced

3 cloves garlic, thinly sliced

½ teaspoon crushed red pepper flakes, or more if you prefer extra heat

3 cups diced tomatoes (about 3 medium)

¾ pound linguine

One 6-ounce jar oil-packed Italian tuna, drained and flaked (I like the Tonnino brand)

½ cup dry white wine, such as a Muscadet or Sauvignon Blanc, or dry vermouth

Freshly ground black pepper

5 ounces baby arugula or other young greens like mustard greens or radish shoots

¼ cup chopped flat-leaf Italian parsley, plus more for serving

Lemon wedges, for serving

1. Bring a large pot of water to a boil. Add 2 tablespoons of the salt and return to a rolling boil.

2. While the water comes to a boil, prepare the sauce: Heat the olive oil in a 12-inch skillet over medium heat. Add the onion and cook until translucent, about 4 minutes. Add the garlic and red pepper flakes and cook until the garlic is pale golden, 2 minutes more. Stir in the tomatoes and cook until they soften, about 5 minutes.

3. Add the linguine to the pot of boiling water and cook until al dente according to package directions.

4. Meanwhile, add the tuna to the sauce and cook for 3 minutes more. Pour in the wine, bring the sauce to a simmer, and cook until the mixture reduces by half, about 3 minutes longer. Season with salt and black pepper.

5. Increase the heat under the skillet to medium-high and scoop the pasta directly into the skillet, tossing to coat. Add the arugula and ½ cup of pasta water, tossing together until the arugula wilts. Sprinkle the parsley over the pasta and toss again, adding ¼ cup of pasta water or more (up to 1 cup), as needed to loosen up the sauce. Season with salt and black pepper.

6. Plate in bowls with parsley and more red pepper flakes, if desired. Serve with lemon wedges for squeezing.

MAMA'S MARINARA

Save this meal to make when you're weary from travel, just moved homes, or anytime you're yearning for something warm and soul filling. This has been my go-to comfort food for as long as I can remember. The sauce requires only four ingredients, which I've been able to find everywhere I've lived. I remove the garlic after it turns to a pale gold so it flavors the oil, but doesn't burn. Then I add it back with the tomatoes. I like to sprinkle lots of grated cheese and black pepper over my portion. **SERVES 4**

Kosher salt

2 tablespoons olive oil

3 cloves garlic, thinly sliced

1 small onion, minced

One 28-ounce can whole or diced San Marzano tomatoes (see Canned Tomatoes, below)

¼ cup chopped flat-leaf Italian parsley, plus more for serving

Freshly ground black pepper

¾ pound cavatappi, or other pasta of your choosing

Grated Pecorino Romano or Grana Padano cheese, for serving

Crushed red pepper flakes (optional)

1. Bring a large pot of water to a boil. Add 2 tablespoons of the salt and return to a rolling boil.

2. While the water comes to a boil, prepare the sauce: Heat the olive oil in a 12-inch skillet over medium heat. Add the garlic and sauté until pale golden, about 2 minutes. Remove the garlic and set aside.

3. Add the onion to the pan and sauté, stirring occasionally, until softened, about 4 minutes. Add the tomatoes to the pan. Fill the tomato can halfway with water, swish the water around, and add it to the pan. Return the garlic to the pan along with the parsley. Season the sauce with salt and black pepper and bring it to a simmer.

4. Add the pasta to the boiling water and cook until al dente according to package directions. Scoop the pasta directly into the skillet and toss to coat, adding ¼ cup of pasta water or more (up to 1 cup), as needed to loosen up the sauce.

5. Serve in bowls with lots of grated Pecorino Romano and, if desired, additional chopped parsley and red pepper flakes.

CANNED TOMATOES For the most part, cans of whole tomatoes and diced tomatoes (a timesaver) can be used interchangeably. Always add tomatoes with their juices, as you'll need their liquid to moisten your sauce. If you're using whole tomatoes, you'll need to break them up, either by gently squeezing them by hand as you add them or in the pan with the back of a spoon. I don't recommend using crushed tomatoes unless specifically requested; I find them too thick for most sauces.

This nutty, hard cheese makes for a perfect pre-dinner snack, served alongside bubbly Lambrusco for sipping.

CRAB FRA DIAVOLO

As boys, my uncles Michael and John often went crabbing in Barnegat Bay off the coast of New Jersey with their cousins. They'd bring back the day's catch to my great-aunt Mary's house, where she would make a marinara sauce, throw in the cleaned crabs, and then serve them straight from the pot with either pasta or bread. This recipe is inspired by their memories; even with shelled crab for ease and hot pepper for kick, the sentiment is the same. **SERVES 4**

¼ cup olive oil

4 cloves garlic, thinly sliced

1 teaspoon crushed red pepper flakes

One 28-ounce can diced San Marzano tomatoes

Kosher salt

Freshly ground black pepper

¾ pound bucatini

¾ pound crabmeat, picked over for bits of shell (Dungeness, blue crab, and jumbo lump crab all work well)

¼ cup chopped flat-leaf Italian parsley, plus more for garnish

¼ cup chopped fresh mint, plus more for garnish

¼ cup chopped fresh chives, plus more for garnish

1. Heat the olive oil in a 12-inch skillet over medium heat. Add the garlic and red pepper flakes and cook until the garlic is pale golden, about 2 minutes.

2. Add the tomatoes and season with salt and black pepper. Reduce the heat to low or medium-low heat and cook the sauce for 20 minutes. While the sauce simmers, bring a large pot of water to a boil. Add 2 tablespoons of the salt and return to a rolling boil. Add the pasta and cook until al dente according to package directions.

3. About 3 minutes before the pasta is done cooking, add the crab and cook until just heated through. Scoop the pasta directly into the skillet and toss to coat. Sprinkle the herbs over the pasta and toss again, adding ¼ cup of pasta water or more (up to 1 cup), as needed to loosen up the sauce. Season with salt and black pepper.

4. Plate in bowls and garnish with additional herbs, if desired.

TOMATO & ZUCCHINI MELT

Whenever my mama would make this dish, we knew it meant that summer had arrived. She would sauté garden tomatoes and zucchini in olive oil until crisp and tender, then she'd tear mozzarella over the vegetables, cover them, and cook them over low heat until the cheese melted. Toss this sauce with pasta and shredded basil to take one of my favorite childhood dishes to another level. When ingredients are this fresh, you don't need much else. **SERVES 4**

Kosher salt

¾ pound penne or other small tubular pasta

2 tablespoons olive oil

2 cloves garlic, thinly sliced

½ teaspoon crushed red pepper flakes

1 large zucchini, about 1 pound, halved lengthwise and cut into ½-inch pieces

½ pound cherry or Sun Gold tomatoes, halved if large

¼ cup torn basil leaves, plus more for garnish

Freshly ground black pepper

¼ cup grated Pecorino Romano cheese, plus more for serving

8 ounces buffalo mozzarella, torn into bite-size pieces

Chopped flat-leaf Italian parsley and mint, optional

1. Bring a large pot of water to a boil. Add 2 tablespoons of the salt and return to a rolling boil. Add the pasta and cook until al dente according to package directions.

2. While the pasta cooks, prepare the sauce: Heat the oil in a 12-inch skillet over medium heat. Add garlic and the red pepper flakes and cook until the garlic is pale golden, about 2 minutes. Add the zucchini and cook for 3 minutes, or until just tender and lightly brown in spots. Stir in the tomatoes and cook until they begin to burst, about 4 minutes more. Add the basil and stir together again. Season to taste with salt and pepper.

3. Add the pasta directly to the skillet and toss to coat. Add the Pecorino Romano and toss again.

4. Plate in bowls and top with mozzarella cheese. Garnish with additional basil, and parsley and mint, if using. Top with additional grated cheese, if desired.

S. [illegible]
W. Cucumber
W.R. Melons Watermelon, WonderBerry, Pumpkin

roccoli   Other
wiss chard   N. Rhubarb

PASTA with YELLOWED CELERY & BEANS

Who doesn't have weeks-old celery at the bottom of their produce drawer waiting for the compost bin at some point? Rather than throwing it out, throw it into a pan with some olive oil, canned tomatoes, and a few other pantry ingredients to coax the most flavor out of this often forgotten ingredient. Here, those yellowed stalks and leaves make for a delicious clean-out-the-fridge sort of dinner. **SERVES 4**

Kosher salt

¾ pound pipe rigate or other small tubular pasta

3 tablespoons olive oil

3 medium stalks celery and leaves (preferably yellow, but fresh works, too), thinly sliced and leaves roughly chopped

1 small onion, chopped

3 cloves garlic, thinly sliced

1 tablespoon chopped fresh oregano, plus more for garnish

One 14.5-ounce can diced San Marzano tomatoes

One 14.5-ounce can white beans, such as cannellini, drained and rinsed

Freshly ground black pepper

¼ cup grated Pecorino Romano cheese, plus more for serving

¼ cup chopped flat-leaf Italian parsley, plus more for garnish

1. Bring a large pot of water to a boil. Add 2 tablespoons of the salt and return to a rolling bowl. Add the pasta and cook until al dente according to package directions.

2. While the pasta cooks, prepare the sauce: Heat the oil in a 12-inch skillet over medium heat. Add the celery and onion and cook until the vegetables soften, about 4 minutes. Add the garlic and oregano and cook for 1 minute more.

3. Increase the heat under the skillet to medium-high and add the tomatoes. Bring to a simmer, then immediately reduce the heat to low. Add the beans and cook until they are heated through, about 3 minutes. Season with salt and pepper.

4. Add the pasta directly to the sauce and toss to coat, adding ¼ cup of pasta water or more (up to 1 cup), as needed to loosen up the sauce. Stir in the Pecorino Romano and parsley and toss again. Season with salt and pepper.

5. Plate in bowls and garnish with additional oregano and parsley. Pass extra grated cheese at the table, if desired.

PASTA E FAGIOLI

Everyone has a different take on this Italian classic that features pasta and beans. Most recipes I've encountered approach this dish like soup. My great-grandmother Colu's recipe, which inspired this one, has more of a stew-like consistency. Arriving in Harrison, New Jersey, at the turn of the century, my great-grandparents didn't have a penny to their name, and so they had to stretch every ingredient. In fact, after cooking the beans for this dish, Colu would save the bean water to make another meal by ladling it over stale Italian bread, drizzling it with olive oil, and adding a generous handful of Pecorino Romano to feed a family of nine. Now, that's back pocket for you! **SERVES 4**

2 tablespoons olive oil, plus more for serving

1 small onion, minced

1 medium carrot, minced

Kosher salt and freshly ground black pepper

One 28-ounce can diced San Marzano tomatoes

½ cup chopped flat-leaf Italian parsley

¼ pound ditalini or other small tubular pasta such as elbows or small shells

One 28-ounce can white beans, such as cannellini, drained and rinsed

2 to 3 cloves garlic, crushed through a garlic press or finely minced

1 cup grated Pecorino Romano cheese, plus more for serving

1. Heat the olive oil in a 6-quart pot over medium heat. Add the onion and carrot and sauté, stirring occasionally, until softened, about 5 minutes. Season with salt and pepper.

2. Add the tomatoes to the pan. Fill the tomato can halfway with water and add the water to the pot. Add half of the parsley, bring the sauce to a simmer, and reduce the heat to low. Simmer the sauce for about 20 minutes, until the flavors have melded. Season with salt and pepper.

3. While the sauce simmers, bring a large pot of water to a boil. Add 2 tablespoons of the salt and bring the water back to a rolling boil. Add the pasta and cook until al dente according to package directions.

4. A few minutes before the pasta is done, add the beans to the sauce and cook until heated through, about 2 minutes more.

5. Add the cooked pasta directly to the pot and toss everything together. Add the crushed garlic, Pecorino Romano, and remaining parsley and toss together again. Season with additional salt and pepper, if desired.

6. Plate in bowls, drizzle with olive oil, and pass grated cheese at the table.

PASTA PUTTANESCA

The name of this pasta cries shelf dinner (and plenty of other scandalous things). After researching the origins of this Italian dish, I still couldn't find a straight answer, but I think we all can agree that it uses many items that one should always have on hand: olives, capers, anchovies, and tomatoes. I've made this for a group of fourteen when traveling through Provence as well as for many a dinner party in Portland, Oregon. It works everywhere, for every palate. **SERVES 4**

2 tablespoons olive oil

3 cloves garlic, thinly sliced

One 2-ounce can anchovy fillets

½ teaspoon crushed red pepper flakes, or more if you like extra heat

1 tablespoon tomato paste

One 28-ounce can diced San Marzano tomatoes

1 cup pitted and halved oil-cured black olives

2 tablespoons capers, rinsed well if salt-packed

1 tablespoon chopped fresh oregano, plus more for garnish

Kosher salt

¾ pound linguine

½ cup chopped flat-leaf Italian parsley, plus more for garnish

1. Bring a large pot of water to a boil.

2. While the water comes to a boil, prepare the sauce: Heat the olive oil in a 12-inch skillet over medium heat. Add the garlic and cook until pale golden, about 2 minutes. Remove the garlic and set aside.

3. Reduce the heat under the skillet to low. Add the anchovies and red pepper flakes and sauté until the anchovies have melted and the red pepper flakes are aromatic, about 1 minute. Add the tomato paste and stir until dissolved. Return the cooked garlic to the pan and stir in the tomatoes. Add the olives, capers, and oregano and allow the sauce to simmer while you cook the pasta.

4. Add 2 tablespoons of the salt to the pot of boiling water and return to a rolling boil. Add the pasta and cook until al dente according to package directions.

5. Add the pasta directly to the sauce and toss to coat, adding ¼ cup of pasta water or more (up to 1 cup), as needed to loosen up the sauce. Add the parsley and toss again.

6. Plate in bowls and garnish with additional oregano and parsley, if desired.

COOK'S NOTE: If you don't have anchovies, use tuna or sardines, or skip the fish altogether! No oil-cured black olives? Use whatever jar of cocktail olives that are hanging around in your fridge. What's important here is a red, salty sauce with some funk—get down and dirty with it.

NONNI'S TUNA-CLAM SAUCE

This dish made a weekly appearance at our family table while I was growing up. My nonni lived with us and, as the water boiled, we would sit around the table and listen to her stories of life in the early 1900s in what she would call "the ghetto," where poor Italian and Irish families who had just immigrated to Newark, New Jersey, lived. I spoke to everyone in our family about the unique addition of tuna to this sauce and no one knows how it came to be. Perhaps it was an inexpensive addition that helped stretch the dish to feed many mouths? Whatever it was, I'm not complaining—it brings pantry pasta with clams to a whole new level. **SERVES 4**

Kosher salt

¼ cup olive oil

4 large cloves garlic, minced

1 tablespoon chopped fresh oregano

One 3-inch-long chile pepper, such as cayenne or serrano, thinly sliced

1 cup clam juice

1 cup chicken broth

¾ pound linguine

One 6- to 7-ounce jar oil-packed Italian tuna (such as Tonnino), drained and flaked

One 6-ounce can clams, drained and chopped (see Cook's Note)

½ cup chopped flat-leaf Italian parsley

Freshly ground black pepper

1. Bring a large pot of water to a boil. Add 2 tablespoons of the salt and return to a rolling boil.

2. While the water comes to a boil, prepare the sauce: Heat the olive oil in a 12-inch skillet over medium heat. Add the garlic and sauté until lightly golden, about 2 minutes. Add the oregano and chile and cook 1 minute more. Add the clam juice and chicken broth, reduce the heat to low, and simmer for 12 minutes, or until the sauce reduces by half.

3. Meanwhile, add the pasta to the boiling water and cook until al dente according to package directions.

4. A few minutes before the pasta is done, increase the heat under the sauce to medium. Stir in the tuna and clams and cook until just heated through, about 3 minutes.

5. Increase the heat to medium-high. Add the pasta directly to the sauce and toss evenly to coat, adding ¼ cup of pasta water or more (up to 1 cup), as needed to loosen up the sauce. Toss in the parsley and season with salt and pepper. Plate in bowls.

COOK'S NOTE: By all means feel free to use fresh clams if you'd prefer them. Simply scrub them clean and steam them open in 1 cup boiling water or wine. Once cooled, removed them from their shells and roughly chop them. Reserve the steaming water for your sauce.

TWO-STEP TORTELLINI en BRODO

On nights when you can't bring yourself to cook, just assemble! I would happily eat this dish any night of the week. It reminds me of when my mama would stroll me over to Raffetto's in the West Village when I was a child, where she would purchase cappelletti or tortellini to take home and simmer in broth for a hearty meal. That chicken stock you have in your freezer or in your pantry? It's time to pull it out. Buy good-quality tortellini stuffed with whatever your pleasure; I prefer meat and cheese. Make a simple salad and toast some bread. You won't be sorry that you cheated while on dinner duty. **SERVES 4**

8 cups chicken stock, preferably homemade

¾ pound fresh cappelletti or tortellini

Grated Pecorino Romano cheese

Flaky salt, such as Maldon or Jacobsen

Freshly ground black pepper

1. Bring the chicken stock to a simmer in a large saucepan. Add the tortellini and cook until al dente according to package directions.

2. Divide the broth and tortellini among bowls and top with a liberal handful of grated Pecorino Romano, flaky salt to taste, and a few generous turns of black pepper.

LINGUINE
con SARDE

This recipe calls for tinned sardines, which are tossed with a simple red sauce and topped with breadcrumbs—they make a protein-packed dish with bright notes thanks to sweet raisins and fennel. I found a version of this dish scrawled in an old notebook my uncle Michael used to record my great-grandmother's and nonni's recipes. The original recipe ends with the note "Serve with haste!" **SERVES 4**

BREADCRUMBS

1 tablespoon olive oil

½ cup panko breadcrumbs

Zest of 1 lemon

¼ cup chopped fennel fronds

Flaky salt, such as Maldon

SAUCE AND PASTA

3 tablespoons olive oil

1 medium fennel bulb, stalks trimmed and reserved for another use (see Cook's Note), halved lengthwise, cored, and thinly sliced

1 small onion, finely chopped

Kosher salt and freshly ground black pepper

3 cloves garlic, finely chopped

½ teaspoon crushed red pepper flakes

One 28-ounce can diced San Marzano tomatoes

½ cup raisins

¾ pound linguine or linguine fini

Two 4-ounce cans oil-packed whole sardines, drained

1. **Prepare the breadcrumbs:** Heat the oil in a 12-inch skillet over low heat. Add the panko and toast until golden, stirring occasionally, about 4 minutes. Remove from the heat and toss with the lemon zest and fennel fronds. Season with salt and set aside.

2. **Make the sauce:** Wipe out the skillet, add the oil, and heat over medium-high heat. Add the fennel and onion and cook, stirring occasionally, until softened, about 4 minutes. Season to taste with salt and black pepper. Add the garlic and red pepper flakes and cook until pale golden, about 2 minutes more.

3. Add the tomatoes and raisins and bring to a simmer. Simmer the sauce for 20 minutes, stirring occasionally. Season with salt and black pepper.

4. **Meanwhile, cook the pasta:** Bring a large pot of water to a boil. Add 2 tablespoons of the kosher salt and return to a rolling boil. Add the pasta and cook until al dente according to package directions.

5. Add the sardines to the sauce and cook for 1 minute, breaking them up to distribute throughout the sauce. Add the pasta directly to the skillet and toss to coat, adding ¼ cup of pasta water or more (up to 1 cup), as needed to loosen up the sauce.

6. Plate in bowls and top with the breadcrumbs.

COOK'S NOTE: My good friend Tamar Adler, the incredible
writer and author of *An Everlasting Meal*, saves the ends
and bits of vegetables and freezes them to make stock or a
makeshift bouquet de garni for braising. Think about items
such as parsley and mushroom stems and the dark green ends
of leeks. Fennel stalks would also be a welcome addition.

SICILIAN ESCAROLE & SAUSAGE

Even though our family is from the Campania region of Italy, the Sicilian mix of pine nuts and raisins makes an appearance in a number of our recipes, including my nonni's braciole. Here that classic combination brings out the sweetness in salty anise-flecked sausage and bitter greens. Although a hearty supper on its own, leftovers the next day call for a fried egg on top (but what isn't better with a little runny yolk?). **SERVES 4**

¼ cup pine nuts

Kosher salt

¾ pound orecchiette

4 tablespoons olive oil

1 pound sweet Italian sausage, casings removed

3 cloves garlic, thinly sliced

1 large head of escarole, cut into 1-inch-wide ribbons

Freshly ground black pepper

⅓ cup raisins, soaked in warm water for 10 minutes, then drained

¼ cup grated Pecorino Romano cheese, plus more for serving

COOK'S NOTE: Italian pine nuts are pricey, but make all the difference in flavor and texture. Freeze what you're not using in a tightly sealed plastic container for up to 3 months.

1. Toast the pine nuts in a 12-inch skillet over medium heat, stirring frequently to make sure they do not burn, until golden, about 3 minutes. Remove and set aside.

2. Bring a large pot of water to a boil. Add 2 tablespoons of the salt and return to a rolling boil. Add the pasta and cook until al dente according to package directions.

3. While the pasta cooks, prepare the sauce: Wipe the skillet you used for the pine nuts clean. Heat 2 tablespoons of the olive oil in the skillet over medium-high heat. Add the sausage and cook until it browns, about 10 minutes, breaking up the meat with the back of a spoon. Remove the sausage and drippings and set aside.

4. Heat the remaining 2 tablespoons oil in the skillet and add the garlic. Sauté until pale golden, about 2 minutes. Begin adding the escarole to the pan, tossing it to wilt until it has cooked down. If needed, add small amounts of pasta water to help it along. Season with salt and pepper.

5. Pour the sausage and drippings back into the pan and toss with the escarole. Add the pasta directly to the sauce along with the raisins and pine nuts and toss to coat, adding ¼ cup of pasta water or more (up to 1 cup), as needed to loosen up the sauce. Add the Pecorino Romano and toss again. Season with salt and pepper, if desired.

6. Plate in bowls and pass grated cheese at the table.

PASTA with MINI MEATBALLS & ESCAROLE

My mama frequently makes her version of "chickarina" soup (aka Italian Wedding Soup). But before you reach for the canned version, take note of how easy this dish is. Here those classic soup ingredients are transformed into heartier fare by forgoing the broth and loading up on pasta. Because the meatballs are small, they cook relatively quickly in the oven. Or make and brown them ahead of time and pop them in the freezer. **SERVES 4**

MEATBALLS

¾ pound ground chicken

2 tablespoons panko breadcrumbs

2 tablespoons grated Pecorino Romano cheese

1 clove garlic, finely chopped

1 large egg, whisked

¼ cup chopped flat-leaf Italian parsley

1 teaspoon kosher salt

PASTA AND SAUCE

Kosher salt and freshly ground black pepper

¾ pound mezze rigatoni

2 tablespoons olive oil

3 cloves garlic, thinly sliced

½ teaspoon crushed red pepper flakes

1 large head of escarole, cut into 1-inch-wide ribbons

¼ cup grated Pecorino Romano cheese, plus more for serving

1. **Prepare the meatballs:** Preheat the oven to 425°F. Line a large baking sheet with foil.

2. In a large bowl and with damp hands, thoroughly combine the chicken, panko, Pecorino Romano, garlic, egg, parsley, and salt. Form the mixture into ½-inch round meatballs (you should end up with about three dozen).

3. Place the meatballs in rows on the baking sheet and bake for 20 to 25 minutes, flipping halfway through to ensure they turn golden on all sides. Remove the baking sheet from the oven and set aside.

4. **Cook the pasta:** Bring a large pot of water to a boil. Add 2 tablespoons of the salt and return to a rolling boil. Add the pasta and cook until al dente according to package directions.

5. **While the pasta cooks, prepare the sauce:** Heat the oil in a 12-inch skillet over medium heat. Add the garlic and red pepper flakes and cook until the garlic is pale golden, about 2 minutes. Add the escarole to the pan, tossing it to wilt until it has cooked down. If needed, add scant ½ cups of pasta water to help it along. Season with salt and black pepper.

6. Increase the heat under the sauce to medium-high. Add the pasta and meatballs directly to the skillet and toss to combine with the escarole, adding ¼ cup of pasta water or more (up to 1 cup), as needed to loosen up the sauce. Stir in the Pecorino Romano and toss again. Plate in bowls with extra grated cheese, if desired.

CREAMY ZUCCHINI & SAUSAGE

By deconstructing my mama's stuffed zucchini recipe, I made it accessible for weeknights when I have no patience for extra steps. The crumbled sausage and a touch of cream make this pasta feel decadent, but the sautéed zucchini keeps it fresh and on the lighter side. It's the smell of rosemary drifting through the house that makes this meal feel extra special. **SERVES 4**

4 small zucchini or 1 large (about 1 pound)

2 tablespoons olive oil

1 pound sweet Italian sausage, casings removed

Kosher salt

¾ pound gigli or campanelle

3 cloves garlic, minced

1 tablespoon chopped fresh rosemary

¼ cup chopped flat-leaf Italian parsley

1 cup diced tomatoes (about 1 medium)

½ cup heavy cream or half-and-half

¼ cup grated Pecorino Romano cheese, plus more for serving

Freshly ground black pepper

1. Bring a large pot of water to a boil.

2. While the water comes to a boil, prepare the sauce: Trim the ends of the zucchini and halve them lengthwise. With a spoon, scoop out the pulp of each half, leaving a ¼-inch shell. Roughly chop the pulp and set aside. Cut the scooped-out zucchini shells crosswise into ¼-inch-thick slices.

3. Heat the oil in a 12-inch skillet over medium heat. Add the sausage and cook until browned, about 7 minutes, breaking up the meat with the back of a wooden spoon. Add 2 tablespoons of the salt to the water and return to a rolling boil. Add the pasta and cook until al dente according to package directions.

4. Add the zucchini pulp, garlic, rosemary, and parsley to the skillet with the sausages and cook together for about 3 minutes. Add the diced tomatoes and cook for 5 minutes more.

5. Stir in the heavy cream and cook for 2 minutes. Stir in the Pecorino Romano.

6. About 30 seconds before the pasta is done, toss the zucchini slices into the boiling water with the pasta. Reserving the pasta water, drain the pasta and zucchini and add them directly to the sauce. Toss the pasta to coat, adding ¼ cup of pasta water or more (up to 1 cup), as needed to loosen up the sauce. Season with salt and pepper, if desired.

7. Plate in a large serving bowl and pass extra Pecorino Romano at the table.

RADIATORE with POTATOES, KALE & BACON

This pasta dish reminds me of the chowder I would always order on Cape Cod as a young girl. Some folks might be put off by a recipe with double the carbs, but I promise that potatoes and pasta tossed with bacon and kale are a heavenly combination.

SERVES 4

Kosher salt

¾ pound baking potatoes, peeled and cut into ⅓-inch dice

¾ pound radiatore or another short corkscrew shape

¼ pound bacon, cut into ½-inch pieces

1 tablespoon olive oil, plus more for drizzling

2 cloves garlic, thinly sliced

1 large bunch lacinato kale or other sturdy greens, tough stems removed (see Cook's Note), leaves cut into 1-inch-wide ribbons

Freshly ground black pepper

Grated Pecorino Romano cheese

Crushed red pepper flakes (optional, but encouraged)

1. Fill a large pot with water and 2 tablespoons of the salt and add the potatoes. When the water comes to a boil, add the pasta and cook until the pasta is al dente and the potatoes are firm-tender, about 10 minutes. Reserving 2 cups of pasta water, drain the pasta and potatoes.

2. While pasta and potatoes cook, prepare the sauce: Add the bacon to a 12-inch skillet and cook over medium-low heat, stirring occasionally, until crisp, about 5 minutes. Remove and set aside on a plate lined with a paper towel. Pour off all but 1 tablespoon of bacon fat.

3. Add the oil to the skillet and heat to medium-low, then add the garlic and cook until pale golden, about 2 minutes. Add the kale and sauté until the kale wilts, about 5 minutes. If needed, add a small amount of pasta water to help the process along. Season with salt and black pepper.

4. Add the pasta and potatoes to the skillet and toss to coat, adding ¼ cup of pasta water or more (up to 1 cup), as needed to loosen up the sauce. You want the sauce to feel slick, but not watered down. Stir in the bacon.

5. Plate in bowls with grated Pecorino Romano, a drizzle of olive oil, and red pepper flakes, if desired.

COOK'S NOTE: I don't remove the ribs from my kale; the crunchy bits don't bother me, and I'm too impatient to take the time to do so. If they bother you, simply remove them by running your knife down each side of the leaf closest to the stem.

CHESTNUT PASTA with RED CABBAGE & PANCETTA

My nonni's braised cabbage, which incorporates red cabbage, cider vinegar, and bacon, is a Thanksgiving dish that we have every year. But it's such a simple recipe that I make it anytime I want—with some added pasta to bring this favorite side to the center of the table. My passion for sherry vinegar took precedence over cider vinegar, and I swapped the bacon for pancetta, but any cured meat will work just fine. **SERVES 4**

Kosher salt

¾ pound chestnut fusilli (see Cook's Note)

2 tablespoons olive oil

6 ounces pancetta, cut into ½-inch pieces

1 medium shallot, thinly sliced

5 cups thinly sliced red cabbage (about ½ medium head)

1 tablespoon roughly chopped fresh sage

2 tablespoons good-quality sherry vinegar

¼ cup grated Grana Padano cheese, plus more for serving

Freshly ground black pepper (optional)

1. Bring a large pot of water to a boil. Add 2 tablespoons of the salt and return to a rolling boil. Add the pasta and cook until al dente according to package directions.

2. While the water comes to a boil, prepare the sauce: Heat the oil in a 12-inch skillet over medium heat. Add the pancetta and cook until crisp, about 4 minutes. Remove and set aside on a plate lined with a paper towel.

3. Reduce the heat under the skillet to medium-low. Add the shallot and cook until it begins to soften, about 4 minutes. Begin adding the cabbage a handful at a time, allowing it to cook down between batches, sautéing until it turns tender and begins to brown, about 5 minutes. Stir in the sage and season with salt. Add the sherry vinegar, stirring to combine until the vinegar evaporates.

4. Add the pancetta and the pasta to the skillet, tossing to combine and adding ¼ cup of pasta water or more (up to 1 cup), as needed to loosen up the sauce. Stir in the Grana Padano. Plate in bowls and sprinkle with additional cheese and fresh black pepper, if desired.

COOK'S NOTE: When the other ingredients in a dish are this simple, it's fun to explore unique pastas such as this one to get out of your comfort zone. Chestnut pasta is made from the flour of ground chestnuts, which adds a nutty flavor to this dish. Look for it at gourmet Italian markets or online. If you can't find it, substitute with farro or whole wheat fusilli.

PASTA with PICKLED PEPPERS

One of my favorite Italian appetizers is pickled cherry peppers stuffed with anchovies, garlic, breadcrumbs, and other odds and ends. I thought it would be fun to deconstruct the dish and serve it over pasta. Our family recipe is quite labor-intensive and includes pickling your own peppers, so I simplified the dish without sacrificing its integrity. The peppers impart an *agrodolce* (sweet and sour) flavor, and the crushed red pepper adds additional heat. **SERVES 4**

BREADCRUMBS

1 tablespoon olive oil

½ cup panko breadcrumbs

1 teaspoon kosher salt

PASTA

Kosher salt

¾ pound spaghettini

¼ cup olive oil, plus more for drizzling

4 cloves garlic, thinly sliced

4 anchovy fillets or 1 tablespoon anchovy paste

½ teaspoon crushed red pepper flakes

1 cup pickled cherry peppers or Peppadew peppers, roughly chopped

Freshly ground black pepper

½ cup chopped flat-leaf Italian parsley

Flaky salt, such as Maldon or Jacobsen, for serving

1. **Prepare the breadcrumbs:** Heat the olive oil in a 12-inch skillet over medium-high heat. Add the breadcrumbs and cook, stirring frequently, until they are golden in color, about 3 minutes. Season with the salt. Remove from the pan and set aside in a small bowl.

2. **Cook the pasta:** Bring a large pot of water to a boil. Add 2 tablespoons of the kosher salt and return to a rolling boil. Add the pasta and cook until al dente according to package directions.

3. **While the pasta cooks, prepare the sauce:** Heat the olive oil in a 12-inch skillet over low heat. Add the garlic and cook until golden, making sure it does not brown, about 2 minutes. Toss in the anchovies and cook until they melt, 1 minute more. Stir in the red pepper flakes and pickled peppers and cook for 2 minutes more. Add a cup of pasta water to the pan, increase the heat to medium, and simmer until the sauce reduces by half, about 2 minutes. Season with salt and black pepper.

4. Increase the heat under the skillet to medium-high and add the pasta directly to the skillet, tossing to coat. Stir in half of the parsley and add ¼ cup of pasta water or more (up to 1 cup), as needed to loosen up the sauce.

5. Plate in bowls and top with the breadcrumbs, remaining parsley, a drizzle of olive oil, and a few flakes of salt.

FRUTTI DI MARE with SQUID INK PASTA

Every Christmas Eve for as long as I can remember, we've gone to Uncle Michael and Aunt Philippa's home to celebrate the Feast of the Seven Fishes. It's my favorite holiday, when everyone digs into (at least) seven Italian dishes, each of which features a different fish or shellfish, such as homemade pizza topped with tuna, egg-and-cheese battered shrimp, *baccalà*, and so much more. We start the day by sitting down to a bowl of Uncle Michael's seafood pasta, which is otherworldly. At a recent gathering, I arrived early so I could make it with him and take notes—just as he did with my nonni for many of her recipes. This celebratory dish calls for something special—so I swapped out typical linguine for its dramatic squid sibling with her inky strands. **SERVES 4**

Kosher salt

1 dozen littleneck clams, scrubbed clean

1 pound mussels, scrubbed clean and beards removed

½ cup white wine

2 tablespoons olive oil

1 small onion, finely chopped

3 cloves garlic, thinly sliced

½ teaspoon crushed red pepper flakes, plus more for serving

One 28-ounce can diced San Marzano tomatoes

½ cup chopped flat-leaf Italian parsley

Freshly ground black pepper

¾ pound squid ink linguine

12 large (16/20 count) shrimp, peeled and deveined

½ pound squid, cleaned and cut into ½-inch-wide rings

1. Bring a large pot of water to a boil. Add 2 tablespoons of the salt and return to a rolling boil.

2. While the water comes to a boil, prepare the sauce: Place the clams and mussels in a large heavy-bottomed saucepan and pour the wine over the shellfish. Set over high heat, cover, and steam the shellfish, shaking the pan occasionally until the shells have opened, about 5 minutes. Remove from the heat and discard any that have not opened. Let cool, then strain the cooking liquid into a bowl and set aside. Remove the sides of the shells that aren't attached to the meat.

3. Wipe out the pan and heat the oil over medium heat. Add the onion and sauté, stirring occasionally, until softened, about 4 minutes. Add the garlic and red pepper flakes and cook until the garlic is pale golden, about 2 minutes more.

4. Add the strained broth from the clams and mussels and cook until it is reduced, 1 minute more. Add the tomatoes and ¼ cup of the parsley and stir together. Fill the tomato can halfway with water, swish it around, and add to the pan. Season with salt and black pepper. Let the sauce simmer while you cook the pasta.

5. Add the pasta to the pot of boiling water and cook until al dente according to package directions.

6. A few minutes before the pasta is done, add the shrimp and squid to the sauce and cook until the shrimp turns pink and the squid turns white and is just cooked through, about 3 minutes.

7. Add the pasta directly to the sauce and toss to coat, adding ¼ cup of pasta water or more (up to 1 cup), as needed to loosen up the sauce. Plate the pasta in bowls, dividing the clams and mussels among the servings, placing them on top. Sprinkle with the remaining ¼ cup parsley and season with additional salt and black pepper, if necessary. Pass red pepper flakes at the table, if desired.

powers street, brooklyn

bright lights, fast dinners

SCALLOPS, SUN GOLDS & A MESS OF HERBS

Bright, candy-colored tomatoes burst open and bring out the sweetness in nutty golden-seared scallops, which are finished with lots of fresh herbs for brightness. To get a good sear on your scallops, make sure the pan gets quite hot. Once they hit the pan, leave them alone to do their thing and flip them just once. **SERVES 4**

Kosher salt

4 tablespoons olive oil

1½ pounds large sea scallops, patted very dry

Freshly ground black pepper

1 shallot, thinly sliced

1 pint baby Sun Gold or grape tomatoes

¾ pound linguine

2 cloves garlic, thinly sliced

½ cup chopped tarragon leaves, plus more for garnish

½ cup chopped flat-leaf Italian parsley, plus more for garnish

½ cup sliced chives (cut at an angle into ½-inch lengths), plus more for garnish

Flaky salt, such as Maldon or Jacobsen, for serving

1. Bring a large pot of water to a boil. Add 2 tablespoons of the kosher salt to the boiling water and return to a rolling boil.

2. While the water comes to a boil, prepare the sauce: Heat 2 tablespoons of the olive oil in a 12-inch skillet over medium-high heat. Season the scallops with salt and pepper and cook until golden brown and opaque, about 3 minutes per side. Transfer them to a plate.

3. Wipe out the skillet, then heat the remaining 2 tablespoons olive oil over low heat. Add the shallot and cook until it begins to caramelize, about 7 minutes. Remove and set aside.

4. Toss the tomatoes into the skillet and cook until they begin to burst, about 8 minutes. Season with salt and pepper.

5. Add the pasta to the pot of boiling water and cook until al dente according to package directions.

6. Stir the garlic and the herbs into the sauce and cook for 2 to 3 minutes. Return the shallots to the skillet, add the pasta, and toss everything together, adding ¼ cup of pasta water or more (up to 1 cup), as needed to loosen up the sauce.

7. Plate the pasta in bowls with 3 or 4 scallops per bowl and garnish with additional herbs and flaky salt.

EASTER HAM CARBONARA

Easter is currently the only holiday I'm "allowed" to host. We cram the whole family (around twenty people) into our 450-square-foot apartment, and I prepare a ham in our tiny kitchen. When it first comes out of the oven we serve it by the slice, and as the day rolls on, we continue picking at it, stuffing it into bread for sandwiches, or rolling it up tightly with mustard. But, let's be honest, Easter ham is never finished on Easter. In the days that follow, I always look forward to ham and eggs, quiche Lorraine, and, of course, split pea soup made with the ham bone—but even after all of that, there is still more ham to be had! I developed this recipe to use up the gift that keeps on giving. I swap out carbonara's traditional pancetta for thickly cut ham and throw in shelled fresh peas right at the end for some color and bite—and as a way to welcome spring. **SERVES 4**

Kosher salt

¾ pound spaghetti

3 eggs plus 1 egg yolk

¾ cup grated Pecorino Romano cheese, plus more for serving

Freshly ground black pepper

2 tablespoons olive oil

5 ounces ham, thickly sliced and cut into ½-inch dice (see Cook's Note)

1 cup shelled fresh peas, or frozen peas

¼ cup chopped flat-leaf Italian parsley

1. Bring a large pot of water to a boil. Add 2 tablespoons of the salt and return to a rolling boil. Add the pasta and cook until al dente according to package directions.

2. While the pasta cooks, prepare the sauce: In a small bowl, whisk together the whole eggs, egg yolk, and Pecorino Romano and season with salt and pepper. Set aside.

3. Heat the olive oil in a 12-inch skillet over medium heat. Add the ham and cook until crisp, about 5 minutes.

4. Reduce the heat to low and add the pasta and ½ cup of pasta water, tossing together to coat. Remove the pan from the heat and add the egg mixture, tossing the pasta rapidly to ensure the egg doesn't scramble.

5. Add the peas and toss again until glossy, adding ¼ cup of pasta water or more (up to 1 cup), as needed to loosen up the sauce.

6. Plate in a large bowl and sprinkle with the parsley. Serve with additional cheese, if desired.

> COOK'S NOTE: Deli sliced ham is too thin for this dish. So if you don't happen to have leftover ham lying around, ask your local butcher for a ham steak.

PRETTY "PARSLIED" SPAGHETTI

My friend Marie La France is the muse behind this meal. Her husband, who owns the Cajun restaurant King Bee in New York's East Village, made this dish for her one lazy Sunday afternoon in New Orleans while they were courting. Parsley and cheese were really the only things left in the fridge, and it became their go-to pasta. Don't be put off by the amount of parsley in this recipe; every strand of spaghetti should be amply covered. **SERVES 4**

Kosher salt

¾ pound spaghetti

2 tablespoons olive oil, plus more for drizzling

4 cloves garlic, thinly sliced

1½ cups finely chopped flat-leaf Italian parsley

1 cup grated Parmesan cheese

Freshly ground black pepper

1. Bring a large pot of water to a boil. Add 2 tablespoons of the salt and return to a rolling boil. Add the pasta and cook until al dente according to package directions.

2. While the pasta cooks, prepare the sauce: Heat the oil in a 12-inch skillet over medium heat. Add the garlic and cook until pale golden, about 2 minutes.

3. Scoop the pasta directly into the skillet with the oil and garlic, tossing to coat. Stir in the parsley and toss until all the strands are covered, adding ¼ cup of pasta water or more (up to 1 cup), as needed to loosen up the sauce. Add the Parmesan and toss again. Salt and pepper the pasta to taste and drizzle with olive oil.

4. Plate in a large bowl and serve with two spoons.

> **COOK'S NOTE:** I kept this recipe true to Marie's story, simple and elegant. However, it's a great canvas for adding anything your heart desires. Some ideas for amping up the oomph include lemon zest; toasted nuts such as hazelnuts, almonds, or walnuts; or sun-dried tomatoes in oil.

TUSCAN KALE "CAESAR" PASTA

I know people want to write off kale because it seems like it's *everywhere* these days, but I still adore its crinkly texture and sweetness. I frequently make kale Caesar salad at home during the week and find that it translates quite well to pasta. You sauté garlic and anchovies in oil and add shredded kale until it cooks down slightly. Finish it off with lots of grated cheese and lemon zest, and (of course!) put an egg on it. **SERVES 4**

BREADCRUMBS

1 tablespoon olive oil

½ cup panko breadcrumbs

Flaky salt, such as Maldon or Jacobsen

PASTA

Kosher salt

¾ pound garganelli or other short tubular pasta

4 tablespoons olive oil

4 eggs

Freshly ground black pepper

4 anchovy fillets or
1 tablespoon anchovy paste

4 cloves garlic, minced

1 large bunch Tuscan kale, tough stems removed, thinly sliced into 1-inch ribbons

¾ cup grated Pecorino Romano or Parmesan cheese, plus more for serving

Zest of 1 lemon

1. **Prepare the breadcrumbs:** Heat the oil in a 12-inch skillet over low heat. Add the breadcrumbs and toast, stirring occasionally, until golden, about 4 minutes. Season with flaky salt and set aside.

2. **Cook the pasta:** Bring a large pot of water to a boil. Add 2 tablespoons of the salt and return to a rolling boil. Add the pasta and cook until al dente according to package directions.

3. **While the pasta cooks, cook the eggs:** Heat 2 tablespoons of the olive oil in a nonstick skillet over medium-high heat. Add the eggs and fry, until the undersides are browned and crispy, 1 to 2 minutes. Season with flaky salt and pepper. Carefully remove and set aside on a plate lined with paper towels.

4. **Prepare the sauce:** Heat the remaining 2 tablespoons oil in a 12-inch skillet over medium heat. Add the anchovies and garlic and cook until the anchovies melt, about 1 minute. Add the kale and season with the salt and pepper. Cook until kale wilts, about 4 minutes, adding ½ cup of pasta water to help it along, if needed.

5. Scoop the pasta directly into the skillet and toss everything together. Add the cheese and toss again, adding ¼ cup of pasta water or more (up to 1 cup), as needed to loosen up the sauce.

6. Plate in bowls and top with the breadcrumbs and lemon zest. Top each bowl with a fried egg. Serve with additional grated cheese, if desired.

PROPOSAL PASTA with ROASTED CHICKEN & MUSHROOMS

Scout's honor, this recipe has nothing to do with Ina Garten's original "Engagement Chicken," but Chad *did* propose after I made this dish. We had hosted friends for a Sunday dinner of roast chicken that I cooked. The next night, craving something creamy and indulgent but also at the mercy of what I had in the apartment, I came home and went to work utilizing the leftover meat. Shortly after we ate, Chad went into the kitchen to prepare homemade ice cream sandwiches (unusual for him, but not suspicious). He walked out of the kitchen and got down on one knee. Seven years later and we're still making this recipe. **SERVES 4**

Kosher salt

¾ pound fettuccine

2 tablespoons olive oil

1 cup thinly sliced shiitake or cremini mushroom caps

1 leek, dark green tops discarded, halved lengthwise and cut crosswise into ¼-inch pieces

3 cloves garlic, thinly sliced

1 fresh red chile pepper, thinly sliced

1 tablespoon chopped fresh sage, plus more for garnish

1 tablespoon roughly chopped fresh thyme, plus more for garnish

Freshly ground black pepper

2 cups shredded roast chicken

1 cup chicken stock

1 cup heavy cream

¼ cup chopped flat-leaf Italian parsley

1. Bring a large pot of water to a boil. Add 2 tablespoons of the salt and return to a rolling bowl. Add the pasta and cook until al dente according to package directions.

2. While the pasta cooks, prepare the sauce: Heat the oil in a 12-inch skillet over medium-high heat. Add the mushrooms, leek, garlic, and chile and cook until softened, about 3 minutes. Stir in the sage and thyme and cook 1 minute more. Season to taste with salt and black pepper.

3. Add the chicken and stir to combine. Pour in the chicken stock, bring to a simmer, and cook until reduced by half, about 3 minutes. Add the cream and cook until the sauce begins to thicken, about 2 minutes.

4. Add the pasta directly to the skillet and toss to combine, adding ¼ cup of pasta water or more (up to 1 cup), as needed to loosen up the sauce. Add the parsley and toss again. Plate in bowls and garnish with sage and thyme.

COOK'S NOTE: Roast chicken will always give you leftovers for another creation, which is why I roast one often. I usually save and refrigerate the drippings, too. As an alternative to using chicken stock in this recipe, scrape off and discard the fat from the demi-glace-like gel that forms on the drippings and add the gel to the pan with some pasta water. It adds an unbeatable richness to the sauce.

MEDITERRANEAN CAVATAPPI

Shape is everything when it comes to enhancing a sauce's texture, so pick your pasta appropriately. For this dish, I chose curlicue cavatappi. With its shorter shape, you'll be sure to fit all the ingredients—artichoke hearts, tomatoes, and olives, too—on your fork. But the best is when you fold in the feta, which melts in the crook of the corkscrews. I top this dish with extra feta and wispy dill, which adds a slightly sweetish grassy flavor. **SERVES 4**

Kosher salt

¾ pound cavatappi

3 tablespoons olive oil

1 pint cherry or grape tomatoes, halved

2 cups oil-packed artichoke hearts, roughly chopped

1 cup sliced pitted kalamata olives

¾ cup roughly chopped dry-packed sun-dried tomatoes

Freshly ground black pepper

7 ounces feta cheese, crumbled

¼ cup finely chopped fresh dill

1. Bring a large pot of water to a boil. Add 2 tablespoons of the salt and return to a rolling boil. Add the pasta and cook until al dente according to package directions.

2. While the pasta cooks, prepare the sauce: Heat the oil in a 12-inch skillet over medium-high heat. Add the cherry tomatoes and cook until they begin to soften, about 4 minutes. Toss in the artichokes, olives, and sun-dried tomatoes and stir together until combined. Cook the sauce for 5 minutes to allow flavors to come together, adding ½ cup of pasta water if the sauce seems dry. Season with salt and pepper.

3. Add the pasta directly to the skillet and toss to coat. Set aside ¼ cup of the feta for garnish and stir the remainder into the skillet, adding ¼ cup of pasta water or more (up to 1 cup), as needed to loosen up the sauce. Toss the pasta again so the cheese begins to melt and the sauce evenly coats the pasta.

4. Plate in bowls and garnish with the reserved feta and the dill. Season with salt and pepper, if desired.

COOK'S NOTE: This recipe was passed down to me from my friend Jenn, whose husband's family has been making it forever. They add chicken to their version, which is a tasty addition! To do so, simply toss some boneless, skin-on thighs in oil, salt and pepper them, then roast in a 375°F oven for 20 to 25 minutes. Let them rest, discard the skin, then shred and add the meat to the sauce before tossing in the pasta.

CACIO E PEPE

With only three ingredients—pasta, pepper, and cheese, which you should always have on hand, by the way—this classic Roman dish comes together in minutes. It's *very* important to use the best-quality ingredients you can find: freshly milled pepper from whole peppercorns and a wedge of sharp, salty Pecorino Romano. Save this dish for those post-event late nights when you get home and realize you had one too many drinks, and that you forgot to eat (not me!). **SERVES 4**

2 tablespoons kosher salt

¾ pound long pasta, such as taglierini, bucatini, or spaghetti

4 tablespoons unsalted butter

2 teaspoons freshly ground black pepper, plus more for serving

1 cup grated Pecorino Romano cheese, plus more for serving

1. Bring a large pot of water to a boil. Add the salt and return to a rolling boil. Add the pasta and cook until al dente according to package directions.

2. When the pasta is about halfway done cooking, start the sauce: Melt the butter in a 12-inch skillet over medium-high heat. Add the pepper and stir until it is aromatic, about 2 minutes. Add ½ cup of the pasta water directly from the pasta pot and bring to a simmer. Stir together and cook for 1 minute, until the sauce emulsifies.

3. Reduce the heat to medium. Add the pasta and Pecorino Romano directly to the skillet, tossing vigorously until all strands are coated and the cheese melts. Add another ½ cup of pasta water and cook for 1 minute more.

4. Plate in bowls with additional grated cheese and black pepper, if desired.

COOK'S NOTE: Purists may object, but I think part of the beauty of this recipe is that you can add to the dish to create interesting variations. I've thrown in roasted broccolini with lemon, nuts, leftover sausage, and other things lying about in my fridge, and they've all worked. Play around and create your own version.

PASTA ALLA ROMAN

One of my favorite perks when I worked at a food magazine was walking downstairs to the test kitchen nearly any time of day to talk about what to make for dinner that evening. My very talented friend Alison Roman would indulge me a few times a week and help me think through my options (and gave me somewhat free rein in the overstocked test kitchen pantry). The one thing we always agreed on: Nearly nothing goes together better than anchovies and pasta.

SERVES 4

Kosher salt

2 tablespoons olive oil

1 tablespoon anchovy paste

½ teaspoon crushed red pepper flakes

3 cloves garlic, thinly sliced

1 cup thinly sliced Vidalia onion

Freshly ground black pepper

One 28-ounce can diced San Marzano tomatoes

¾ pound bucatini or other long, thin pasta

¼ cup chopped flat-leaf Italian parsley, plus more for garnish

Grated Pecorino Romano cheese, for serving

1. Bring a large pot of water to a boil. Add 2 tablespoons of the salt and return to a rolling boil.

2. While the water comes to a boil, prepare the sauce: Heat the oil in a 12-inch skillet over medium-high heat. Add the anchovy paste, red pepper flakes, and garlic and cook until fragrant, about 2 minutes. Add the onion and cook until softened, stirring occasionally, about 4 minutes. Season with salt and pepper.

3. Stir in the tomatoes. Bring the sauce to a simmer and cook for 20 minutes, stirring often.

4. While sauce simmers, cook the pasta: Add the pasta to the pot of boiling water and cook until al dente according to package directions.

5. Increase the heat under the sauce to medium-high. Add the pasta directly to the skillet and toss to coat, adding ¼ cup of pasta water or more (up to 1 cup), as needed to loosen up the sauce. Add the parsley and toss the pasta again.

6. Plate in bowls and top with grated Pecorino Romano and salt and black pepper. Garnish with additional parsley, if desired.

LINGUINE with QUICK CHILI OIL & CAPERS

Most of us always have crushed red pepper flakes and capers on hand. (If not, then it's time to restock your kitchen.) Both of these reliable ingredients have a long shelf life and can take a dish from "eh" to "oh!" This chili oil doesn't take long to make but still packs a punch, while the capers and lemon keep things briny and fresh. **SERVES 4**

Kosher salt

¾ pound linguine

¼ cup olive oil

4 cloves garlic, thinly sliced

½ tablespoon crushed red pepper flakes

3 tablespoons capers, rinsed well if salt-packed

Zest and juice of 1 large lemon

¼ cup grated Pecorino Romano cheese, plus more for serving

¼ cup chopped flat-leaf Italian parsley, plus more for garnish

Freshly ground black pepper

1. Bring a large pot of water to a boil. Add 2 tablespoons of the salt and return to a rolling boil. Add the pasta and cook until al dente according to package directions.

2. While the pasta cooks, prepare the sauce: Heat the oil in a 12-inch skillet over medium-low heat. Add the garlic and red pepper flakes and cook until the oil turns a reddish brown, about 3 minutes.

3. Increase the heat under the skillet to medium. Add the capers, lemon zest, and lemon juice and cook together for 2 minutes. Add ½ cup of pasta water to the pan and cook 2 minutes more.

4. Add the pasta directly to the skillet and toss to coat, adding ¼ cup of pasta water or more (up to 1 cup), as needed to loosen up the sauce. Add the grated Pecorino Romano and parsley to the pan and cook the pasta for 1 minute more.

5. Plate in bowls, season with salt and black pepper, and top with additional Pecorino Romano and parsley.

BRUSSELS SPROUTS
with WHOLE-GRAIN MUSTARD

My friend Sue Li, who is a food stylist, is seriously kick-ass in the kitchen. But even though inspiring ingredients surround her all day, surprisingly, she typically comes home to an empty fridge. Cooking at home is sometimes the last thing she wants to do; she admits that many times the thought of having to wash another pan makes her want to cry. We've all been there! On those days, she just wants something simple and homemade—not takeout, not another dash of hot sauce or fish sauce—so she scrounges around her cabinets and cobbles together a servable amount of spaghetti from almost-empty boxes, scoops out the last bit of mustard, and crisps up whatever veggies are left—dinner is done! **SERVES 4**

Kosher salt

¾ pound spaghetti or other long, thin pasta

2 tablespoons olive oil

1 clove garlic, thinly sliced

½ pound Brussels sprouts, trimmed and pulled apart into leaves (about 6 cups)

Freshly ground black pepper

4 tablespoons unsalted butter

3 tablespoons whole-grain mustard

¼ cup grated Pecorino Romano cheese, plus more for serving

1. Bring a large pot of water to a boil. Add 2 tablespoons of the salt and return to a rolling boil. Add the pasta and cook until al dente according to package directions.

2. While the pasta cooks, heat the oil in a 12-inch skillet over medium-high heat. Add the garlic and cook until golden, about 2 minutes. Working in batches of about 2 cups at a time, add the Brussels sprouts leaves and cook until the edges of the leaves are browned. Transfer the leaves to a bowl as they are cooked. Repeat until all the Brussels sprouts are cooked, about 5 minutes. Season with salt and pepper in the bowl.

3. Wipe out the pan and melt the butter over medium heat. Stir in the mustard, Pecorino Romano, and about ½ cup of pasta water, swirling the pan to emulsify the sauce. Scoop the pasta directly into the skillet along with the Brussels sprouts and toss to coat, adding ¼ cup of pasta water or more (up to 1 cup), as needed to loosen up the sauce.

4. Plate in bowls and top with a generous amount of black pepper and more Pecorino Romano.

COOK'S NOTE: This recipe will work well with just about any nut, so feel free to use whatever you have lying around, such as almonds or pecans. No radicchio? Another bitter leafy green like curly endive or Dandelion greens are a great substitute.

Penne rigate is similar in shape and size to penne, but it has deep ridges, which hold more sauce, maximizing the amount of creaminess in each bite!

PENNE RIGATE with GORGONZOLA, RADICCHIO & WALNUTS

You've got everything you need here for a successful dinner: a little sweet, something bitter, and some crunch. The Gorgonzola adds a silky texture and curbs the gentle bite of the radicchio. Walnuts add, well, nuttiness and are a traditional northern Italian combination with the other two ingredients at play. If you have a blood orange around, grate some zest over the top for brightness and then garnish with chopped parsley. This can work well as a starter to a Sunday roast or as a main alongside a quick green salad. **SERVES 4**

1 cup chopped walnuts

Kosher salt

¾ pound penne rigate

¼ cup olive oil

1 head (about 1 pound) radicchio (preferably Treviso if you can find it), cut into 1-inch-wide ribbons

Freshly ground black pepper

6 ounces crumbled Gorgonzola or other mild blue cheese

½ cup chopped flat-leaf Italian parsley

Orange zest (preferably from a blood orange; optional)

Grated Pecorino Romano cheese, for serving

1. Heat a 12-inch skillet over medium heat. Add the walnuts and toast them over medium-low heat for about 4 minutes, stirring frequently so they do not burn. Remove and set aside. Wipe out the skillet.

2. Bring a large pot of water to a boil. Add 2 tablespoons of the salt and return to a rolling boil. Add the pasta and cook until al dente according to package directions.

3. While the pasta cooks, prepare the sauce: Heat the oil in a 12-inch skillet over medium-high heat. Add the radicchio and season with salt and pepper. Cook the radicchio until it begins to wilt and brown, about 5 minutes. Season with salt and pepper.

4. Stir in the Gorgonzola and cook for 2 minutes. Add ½ cup of the pasta water directly from the pot and simmer for 3 minutes more. The water should emulsify the cheese and create a velvety texture.

5. Scoop the cooked pasta directly into the skillet and toss to combine the pasta with the sauce. Add the walnuts and parsley and toss again until glossy, adding ¼ cup of pasta water or more (up to 1 cup), as needed to loosen up the sauce.

6. Plate in bowls and garnish with orange zest, if desired. Season with salt and pepper and pass grated Pecorino Romano.

QUICK SAUSAGE SUGO

My husband, Chad, is a red-sauce kind of guy, which usually means he wants meat in there, too. I don't have time to make a Sunday sauce during the week, so this recipe uses uncased Italian sausage, which already has great seasoning, allowing you to cut some of the simmering time without sacrificing flavor. Buy the best-quality sausage you can for this recipe—it makes all the difference. Often I'll mix sweet and spicy sausage, but pick according to your preference. **SERVES 4**

1 medium leek (white and light green parts only), roughly chopped

1 medium carrot, cut into 1-inch pieces

1 celery stalk, roughly chopped

2 cloves garlic

2 tablespoons olive oil

1½ pounds sweet or hot Italian sausage, casings removed

Kosher salt

Freshly ground black pepper

1 tablespoon roughly chopped fresh rosemary

1 tablespoon roughly chopped fresh thyme

1 tablespoon tomato paste

One 28-ounce can diced or whole San Marzano tomatoes

½ cup chopped flat-leaf Italian parsley leaves

¾ pound rigatoni or other large tubular pasta

Grated Pecorino Romano cheese, for serving

1. In a food processor, pulse together the leek, carrot, celery, and garlic. Set aside.

2. Heat the oil in a 12-inch skillet over medium-high heat. Add the sausage and cook until browned, about 10 minutes, breaking up the meat with the back of a wooden spoon. Remove from the skillet and set aside. Pour off all but 2 tablespoons of fat.

3. Reduce the heat to medium. Add the vegetables to the pan and sauté until they are golden in color and begin to caramelize, about 7 minutes. Season with salt and pepper. Return the sausage to the pan and stir to combine. Add the rosemary and thyme cook 1 minute more.

4. Stir in the tomato paste and then add the tomatoes. Fill the tomato can halfway with water, slosh around, and add the water to the pan. Stir in the parsley. Bring the sauce to a simmer and cook for 30 minutes.

5. While the sauce simmers, cook the pasta: Bring a large pot of water to a boil. Add 2 tablespoons of the salt and return to a rolling boil. Add the pasta and cook until al dente according to package directions. Meanwhile, check your sauce, adding a small amount of pasta water to the sauce if it appears dry.

6. Add the pasta directly to the skillet and toss together, adding ¼ cup of pasta water or more (up to 1 cup), as needed to loosen up the sauce.

7. Plate in bowls and top with any extra sauce that remains in the pan and pass grated Pecorino Romano at the table.

LINGUINE with SAVOY CABBAGE & SALUMI

The most delicious dinners are sometimes born of necessity rather than creativity. A few years ago, we were leaving for vacation and I was in clean-out-the-fridge mode. I found three ingredients: scraps from a leftover *salumi* platter, a head of savoy cabbage, and some Parmesan cheese. The result was magic. Make sure to garnish this with lots of additional cheese, a drizzle of olive oil, and a few good turns of the pepper mill.

SERVES 4

Kosher salt

¾ pound linguine

2 tablespoons olive oil, plus more for drizzling

4 ounces thinly sliced salumi (salami, soppressata, or prosciutto work well; a combination of all three is nice, but not necessary)

¾ pound savoy cabbage, cored and thinly sliced (about 6 cups)

Freshly ground black pepper

½ cup grated Parmesan, plus more for serving

1. Bring a large pot of water to a boil. Add 2 tablespoons of the salt and return to a rolling boil. Add the pasta and cook until al dente according to package directions.

2. While the pasta cooks, prepare the sauce: Heat the oil in a 12-inch skillet over medium heat. Add the salumi and cook until crisp, about 3 minutes. Remove and set aside.

3. Add the cabbage, season with salt and pepper, and sauté until the cabbage wilts, about 7 minutes. Return the salumi to the pan with any fat that has accumulated.

4. Scoop the pasta directly into the skillet and toss together to coat, adding ¼ cup of pasta water or more (up to 1 cup), as needed to loosen up the sauce. Add the Parmesan cheese and toss again.

5. Plate in bowls with black pepper and a drizzle of olive oil. Pass additional Parmesan cheese at the table.

ROTINI with CARAMELIZED ONIONS, FETA & WALNUTS

I love to make this dish early in the fall when I feel a chill in the air—it's the ultimate comfort food. Make sure to give the onions enough time to cook slowly so they sweeten and soften and turn deeply golden. The salty feta, which you toss in at the end, gently melts, but still keeps some of its structure. You can use whatever herbs you find in the fridge, but oregano and flat-leaf Italian parsley are always a must. Thyme and sage work well, too. If you're feeling extra indulgent, add a spoonful of fresh ricotta before serving (not necessary, but, oh, so good). **SERVES 4**

¼ cup olive oil

3 large yellow onions, halved and thinly sliced

3 large red onions, halved and thinly sliced

2 tablespoons unsalted butter (optional)

1 tablespoon chopped fresh oregano, plus more for garnish

Kosher salt

Freshly ground black pepper

1 cup chopped walnuts

¾ pound rotini or fusilli

8 ounces feta cheese, crumbled

¼ cup chopped flat-leaf Italian parsley, plus more for garnish

1. Heat the olive oil in a 12-inch skillet over medium-low heat. Add the onions and cook slowly, stirring often, until they caramelize, about 45 minutes. Add the butter to help them brown if necessary. Add the oregano to the onions and season with salt and pepper.

2. While the onions are cooking, heat a small skillet over low heat and toast the chopped walnuts, about 4 minutes. Remove and set aside.

3. When the onions are about halfway done cooking (about 20 minutes), bring a large pot of water to a boil. Add 2 tablespoons of the salt and return to a rolling boil. Add the pasta and cook until al dente according to package directions.

4. Scoop the pasta directly into the skillet with the caramelized onions and toss to coat. Add the feta, walnuts, parsley, and ¼ cup of pasta water. Toss together until the cheese begins to melt, adding an additional ¼ cup of pasta water or more (up to 1 cup), as needed to loosen up the sauce.

5. Plate in bowls and garnish with oregano, parsley, and salt and pepper, if desired.

COOK'S NOTE: Because caramelizing onions takes a little time, I recommend doing this step on a Sunday to set yourself up for the week. Make a big batch to use as a topping for pizza or burgers, in a frittata, on toast with ricotta and herbs. The caramelized onions store well in the fridge and can also be easily reheated on the stove over low heat.

RIGATONI with ROASTED CAULIFLOWER & CRISPY CAPERS

I'll eat cauliflower prepared any way, but something about roasting it brings out its nuttiness, which brings me to my knees. If you spot purple or "cheddar" cauliflower at the market, snatch them for this recipe! Their vivid colors (especially if you use two or three varieties) make this dish a sight for sore eyes. Make sure to crisp those capers for extra crunch. **SERVES 4**

1 head cauliflower, cored and cut into small florets

⅓ cup olive oil

Kosher salt

Freshly ground black pepper

Flaky salt, such as Maldon or Jacobsen

¾ pound rigatoni or other tubular pasta

3 tablespoons capers, rinsed well if salt-packed

3 cloves garlic, thinly sliced

½ teaspoon crushed red pepper flakes, or more to taste

Zest of 1 lemon

½ cup chopped flat-leaf Italian parsley

Grated Parmesan or Pecorino Romano, for serving

1. Preheat the oven to 450°F.

2. In a large bowl, toss the cauliflower florets with 2½ tablespoons of the oil and season with kosher salt and black pepper. Arrange the florets in a single layer on a large rimmed baking sheet and roast them, tossing occasionally, until deeply golden in color, about 25 to 30 minutes. Sprinkle with flaky salt. Remove and set aside.

3. Bring a large pot of water to a boil. Add 2 tablespoons of the kosher salt and return to a rolling boil. Add the pasta and cook until al dente according to package directions.

4. When the pasta is about 5 minutes from being done, heat the remaining olive oil in a 12-inch skillet over medium-high heat. Add the capers and cook until they begin to crisp, about 3 minutes. Reduce the heat to medium, add the garlic, and cook until golden, about 2 minutes. Stir in the red pepper flakes and cook for 1 minute more.

5. Increase the heat to medium-high and add the pasta, roasted cauliflower, lemon zest, and parsley and toss to coat, adding ¼ cup of pasta water or more (up to 1 cup), as needed to loosen up the sauce. Season with kosher salt and black pepper.

6. Plate in bowls and top with grated cheese.

FUSILLI ALFREDO

This recipe comes from one of my dearest friends, Carla Lalli Music. We met while working together and discovered that her family also hails from Avellino, a small province outside of Naples, so we developed an immediate kinship. Alfredo is her favorite back pocket pasta. "My mom cooked this for me most Saturday nights when I was growing up, and I used to throw my body over the bowl to keep my dad from eating half of it out of my plate (then I'd yell at him to stop eating it straight out of the pot)," Carla told me. Her recipe is a true Alfredo, which means no cream, milk, or flour. The sauce is a glossy emulsion of butter and starchy pasta water, which she finishes with lots of black pepper, like you would a carbonara. "Whoever you make this for will know instantly that you love them very much. At least, that's what it tastes like to me." Spoken in true Carla fashion. **SERVES 4**

Kosher salt

¾ pound fusilli pasta

8 tablespoons (1 stick) unsalted butter, cut into a few pieces

¾ cup finely grated Parmesan cheese (but not Microplaned), plus more for serving

Freshly ground black pepper

> **COOK'S NOTE:** Carla recommends using the smallest holes on a box grater, as the Microplane can make the cheese too fluffy and it has a tendency to make stuff gloppy when it melts, instead of "coat-y." Alternately, you can blitz it in a food processor until the cheese forms very small beads.

1. Bring a large pot of water to a boil. Add 2 tablespoons of the salt and return to a rolling boil. Add the pasta and cook until al dente according to package directions. Reserving 1½ cups of the pasta cooking liquid, drain the pasta and let sit in a colander while you prepare the sauce. (I know I usually don't drain the pasta, but in this one case I make an exception because it's Carla's recipe and I trust her implicitly when it comes to cooking.)

2. Return the pasta pot to medium heat and add the pasta cooking liquid. When it comes to a simmer, gradually whisk the butter into the pasta water, one piece at a time, waiting until one piece melts before adding another. Once you've added all of the butter, the sauce should look creamy and glossy, not greasy and broken. (It will seem pretty thin, and you might worry that it is too loose, but fear not.)

3. Gradually whisk in the Parmesan, adding it by the handful and making sure it has melted before adding more. Return the pasta to the pot and toss rapidly until all the noodles are coated and the sauce has thickened somewhat.

4. Plate in bowls topped with a few grinds of black pepper and more Parmesan cheese, if desired.

CREAMY SAFFRON RISOTTO-STYLE FREGOLA

This recipe comes from my sweet friend Jen, who also happens to be half of Peden + Munk, the incredible photo team on this book. From the young age of three, Jen would beg her mom for kitchen tasks. They often included making coffee, rolling dough, or pouring drinks. Years later while in college, she rented a kitchen-less guesthouse in Pasadena. Luckily, it did have an outdoor grill and she attempted to be creative with the little resources she had. But eventually, doing dishes in the bathroom sink became too much. Then Jen met Taylor Peden, who happened to have a kitchen. On their first date they made chicken Marsala, she burned her fingertips, and they fell in love. Jen knew she had met her match. To this day they cook together almost every day, often alongside her mother-in-law, Paulette, whom I also adore, and who inspired this recipe. **SERVES 4**

5 cups chicken stock, preferably homemade

2 tablespoons olive oil

4 slices prosciutto

2 medium shallots, minced

Pinch of saffron threads

¾ pound fregola

½ cup white wine

3 tablespoons unsalted butter, at room temperature

½ cup grated Pecorino Romano cheese, plus more for serving

Freshly ground black pepper

1. Bring the chicken stock to a simmer in a large saucepan. You may not need to use all 5 cups, but it's good to have it ready, just in case you do.

2. Meanwhile, heat the oil in a separate large, heavy-bottomed saucepan over medium heat. Add the prosciutto to the pan and cook for 3 minutes or until crisp. Remove from the pan and set aside on a plate lined with paper towels.

3. Add the shallots to the pan and cook over medium heat until soft and translucent, about 4 minutes, making sure they do not brown.

4. Combine ½ cup of stock and the saffron in a measuring cup with a spout. Stir, cover, and set aside.

5. Add the fregola to the pan of shallots, stirring to coat the pasta. Add the wine to deglaze the pan and scape up any browned bits. Continue cooking until the liquid reduces by half, about 2 minutes.

(recipe continues)

COOK'S NOTE: Jen often serves this as a side to osso buco or other braised meats, but I think it makes a wonderful meal on its own.

6. Stir in 1 cup of hot stock. Cook, stirring constantly until the pasta has absorbed most of the stock. Continue stirring and adding stock 1 cup at a time, allowing the pasta to absorb the stock before adding more, until the pasta is almost tender, about 15 minutes. Just as the pasta becomes tender, add the reserved saffron stock.

7. Remove the pan from the heat and stir in the butter and Pecorino Romano. Let the pasta rest for 3 minutes. Plate in warm bowls topped with the crispy prosciutto, more Pecorino Romano, and a few turns of black pepper.

ROTINI with RAINBOW CHARD & ORANGE-FENNEL RICOTTA

Having a bottle of dry vermouth in your pantry is as good as gold for taking pasta to the next level and breaking out of your weeknight cooking rut. It keeps longer than white wine, and it's easy on the budget. It's also a great way to deglaze a pan and coax the sweetness out of your ingredients—for both tomato- and cream-based sauces. For this recipe, Swiss chard braises in vermouth, and the ricotta, which you add at the end, coats the pasta for a creamy herbal sauce. Orange zest and toasted fennel seeds bring out the aromatics of the vermouth and give the dish great character. **SERVES 4**

¼ cup ricotta cheese

Zest of ½ orange

1 tablespoon fennel seeds, crushed

Kosher salt

Freshly ground black pepper

¾ pound rotini

3 tablespoons olive oil

2 large bunches rainbow chard, stems removed, leaves cut into ½-inch-wide ribbons

3 cloves garlic, thinly sliced

½ teaspoon crushed red pepper flakes

1 cup dry vermouth or white wine

¼ cup grated Grana Padano or Parmesan cheese

1. In a small bowl, stir together the ricotta and orange zest.

2. Toast the fennel seeds in a 12-inch skillet over medium heat until aromatic, stirring frequently to make sure they do not burn, about 3 minutes. Remove the seeds and stir them into the ricotta-orange mixture. Season with salt and black pepper. Set aside and wipe the skillet clean.

3. Bring a large pot of water to a boil. Add 2 tablespoons of the salt and return to a rolling boil. Add the pasta and cook until al dente according to package directions.

4. While the pasta cooks, prepare the sauce: Heat the oil in the skillet over medium-high heat. Add the rainbow chard and sauté for about 4 minutes, or until the leaves begin to soften. Add the garlic and red pepper flakes and cook for 2 minutes more. Add the vermouth and cook until the chard begins to cook down and the mixture has reduced by half, 3 to 5 minutes. Season with salt and black pepper.

5. Add the pasta and cheese directly to the skillet and toss to coat, adding ¼ cup of pasta water or more (up to 1 cup), as needed to loosen up the sauce.

6. Plate in bowls and place a spoonful of ricotta on top of each serving. Season with salt and black pepper, if desired.

SPAGHETTI ANTALINA

My fellow Napolitano paisano Seth Bodie introduced me to this southern Italian dish that combines anchovies, walnuts, chiles, and lots of garlic and parsley. His family serves this as part of their Feast of the Seven Fishes on Christmas Eve; we've been eating it together since our early days in New York City, when we were fresh out of college and the simplest pantry pasta felt like a luxury—easy on our wallets and heavy in our bellies. It's still one of my favorites. **SERVES 4**

BREADCRUMBS

1 tablespoon olive oil

½ cup panko breadcrumbs

Flaky salt, such as Maldon or Jacobsen

PASTA

Kosher salt

¾ pound spaghetti

1 cup chopped walnuts

¼ cup olive oil

4 cloves garlic, chopped

One 2-ounce can anchovy fillets

1 teaspoon crushed red pepper flakes

¾ cup chopped flat-leaf Italian parsley

Freshly ground black pepper

Grated Pecorino Romano cheese, for serving

1. **Toast the breadcrumbs:** Heat the oil in a 12-inch skillet over low heat. Add the panko and toast until golden, stirring occasionally, about 4 minutes. Season with flaky salt and set aside.

2. **Cook the pasta:** Bring a large pot of water to a boil. Add 2 tablespoons of the salt and return to a rolling boil. Cook the pasta until al dente according to package directions.

3. **While the pasta cooks, prepare the sauce:** Heat a 12-inch skillet and toast the walnuts over medium heat, about 4 minutes. Remove and set aside. Wipe out the skillet.

4. Heat the olive oil in the skillet over medium-high heat. Add the garlic and cook until lightly golden, about 2 minutes. Stir in the anchovies and cook until they melt, about 2 minutes. Add the red pepper flakes and cook 1 minute more.

5. Scoop the pasta directly into the skillet and toss with the anchovy mixture. Toss in the walnuts and parsley and mix together until everything is combined, adding ¼ cup of pasta water or more (up to 1 cup), as needed to loosen up the sauce.

6. Plate in bowls and top with the breadcrumbs. Season with salt and black pepper, if desired. Pass the Pecorino Romano at the table.

SMOKY GARGANELLI ALLA VODKA

Who doesn't love an easy-to-assemble Italian-American classic? Plus, who doesn't have a bottle of vodka tucked away in their freezer for when the Russian side of the family visits? (I'm always prepared for when my cousin-in-law Igor comes by!) No matter where you're from, this comforting dish will please—and to bring out its retro Italian vibes, serve this with Caesar salad, garlic bread, and Chianti. Cue the Sinatra. **SERVES 4**

Kosher salt

¾ pound garganelli or penne

2 tablespoons olive oil

1 medium yellow onion, minced

2 cloves garlic, chopped

4 ounces 'nduja (see Cook's Note), optional

¾ cup vodka

One 28-ounce can crushed San Marzano tomatoes

Freshly ground black pepper

¾ cup heavy cream

¼ cup grated Grana Padano or Parmesan cheese, plus more for serving

2 tablespoons roughly chopped fresh oregano

2 tablespoons roughly chopped flat-leaf Italian parsley

1. Bring a large pot of water to a boil. Add 2 tablespoons of the salt and return to a rolling boil. Add the pasta and cook until al dente according to package directions.

2. While the pasta cooks, prepare the sauce: Heat the oil in a 12-inch skillet over medium heat. Add the onion and cook until translucent, about 3 minutes. Add the garlic and cook 1 minute more. Add the 'nduja (if using) and cook, stirring until it begins to melt, about 2 minutes.

3. Add the vodka to skillet and cook for 2 minutes more to reduce by half. Stir in the tomatoes and simmer for 10 minutes. Season with salt and pepper. Reduce the heat to low, stir in the cream, and cook 1 minute more.

4. Add the pasta and grated cheese directly to the skillet and toss to coat.

5. Plate in bowls and top with the oregano and parsley. Top with additional cheese and salt and pepper, if desired.

COOK'S NOTE: I upped the ante here by including 'nduja, a spicy, spreadable salami from Calabria, for some heat; for a meat-free dish, substitute straightforward red pepper flakes. You'll lose the smokiness of the dish, but it will still taste great.

BACCALÀ & GREEN OLIVE PASTA with ALMONDS

I met Rebecca Jurkevich for the first time at a photo shoot in Napa and was immediately impressed by her work. She is such an incredibly gifted food stylist and cook, and I was so grateful she agreed to work with me on this book. (I mean, look at these pastas.) She asked me if I had any recipes that included salt cod (or *baccalà*) and I shook my head no. I had forgotten all about this pantry staple! The salt preserves the cod, lending it a long shelf life, and other than a long bath, the cod needs no special care. Rebecca generously came up with this recipe, which I am so happy to share with you. **SERVES 4**

1 pound salt cod

2 tablespoons kosher salt

¾ pound spaghetti

½ cup blanched almonds, roughly chopped

¼ cup olive oil

4 cloves garlic, thinly sliced

2 serrano chile peppers, thinly sliced

½ cup roughly chopped pitted Castelvetrano or other green olives

¼ cup fresh lemon juice

½ cup dry white wine or dry vermouth

½ cup roughly chopped flat-leaf Italian parsley

1. The day before you plan to make this recipe, soak the salt cod in water for 24 hours, changing the water about every 6 hours.

2. Rinse the cod. Place it in a large pot and cover by 1 inch of water. Bring to a boil, reduce to a simmer, and cook until the fish easily flakes apart, 30 to 40 minutes.

3. About 20 minutes before the cod is finished, bring a large pot of water to a boil. Add the salt and return to a rolling boil. Add the pasta and cook until al dente according to package directions.

4. While the pasta cooks, prepare the sauce: Toast the chopped almonds in a 12-inch skillet over medium heat, stirring occasionally to make sure they do not burn, about 3 minutes. Remove and set aside.

5. Wipe out the pan and heat the oil over medium heat. Add the garlic and cook until pale golden, about 2 minutes. Add the chiles, olives, and lemon juice and stir to combine, cooking 2 minutes more. Add the white wine, bring to a simmer, and reduce the sauce by half, about 2 minutes. Add the fish and half of the parsley to the skillet and toss to combine.

6. Add the pasta directly to the pan, adding ¼ cup of pasta water or more, tossing to coat. Plate in bowls with the remaining parsley and top with the toasted almonds.

CREAMED SPINACH PASTA

My friends Leslie, Meghan, and Nikki and I had a tradition of dining at Keens Steakhouse in Manhattan every time someone reached a career milestone. We called it our International Women's Business Lunch (read: martinis). Creamed spinach is my guilty pleasure at these beloved lunches, and it got me thinking about creating a pasta dish that plays on those ingredients. This luxurious sauce feels celebratory to me and would be a comforting dinner on a cold winter night. Serve with bubbles! **SERVES 4**

¾ cup ricotta cheese

Kosher salt

Freshly ground black pepper

¾ pound long pasta such as tagliatelle or fettuccine

½ cup pine nuts

4 tablespoons unsalted butter

2 cloves garlic, thinly sliced

1 pound baby spinach leaves

1 cup heavy cream

Freshly grated nutmeg

Grated Pecorino Romano cheese, for serving

1. In a large bowl, combine the ricotta with salt and pepper to taste. Set aside.

2. Bring a large pot of water to a boil. Add 2 tablespoons of the salt and return to a rolling boil. Add the pasta and cook until al dente according to package directions.

3. While the pasta cooks, prepare the sauce: Toast the pine nuts in a 12-inch skillet over medium heat, stirring occasionally to make sure they do not burn, about 3 minutes. Remove and set aside.

4. Wipe the skillet clean and melt the butter over medium-low heat. Add the garlic and sauté until pale golden, about 2 minutes. Add the spinach and cook down until it wilts, about 4 minutes more.

5. Add the cream, bring to a simmer, and cook until the sauce begins to thicken slightly, about 2 minutes. Season with salt, pepper, and nutmeg.

6. Scoop the pasta directly into the skillet and toss to combine. Add the pasta and spinach mixture to the bowl of ricotta off the heat and toss to coat, adding ¼ cup of pasta water or more (up to 1 cup), as needed to loosen up the sauce.

7. Plate in bowls and sprinkle with the pine nuts. Season with salt and pepper, if desired. Pass grated Pecorino Romano at the table.

hudson & the valley

farm visits and market meals

RAMP & HAZELNUT PESTO

I'll admit it, I am just like the hundreds of thousands of New Yorkers who wait and wait all year for those very few weeks when ramps make their VIP appearance at the Union Square Greenmarket. When I'm in Hudson, I'm lucky enough to live by my friends Mimi and Richard Beaven's Little Ghent Farm, where I forage for my own. I crouch down low and pull them from the earth and rush home to parcel them out for different meals. For this one, I blanch the ramps first so they stay bright green, and use hazelnuts for their creamy and buttery flavor. No hazelnuts? No problem. Toasted almonds work well, too. **SERVES 4**

Kosher salt

4 ounces ramps, leaves separated from the stems and bulbs

¾ pound campanelle

¼ cup hazelnuts, toasted and skins removed

⅓ cup olive oil, plus more as needed

5 tablespoons grated Pecorino Romano cheese

Freshly ground black pepper (optional)

1. Bring a large pot of water to a boil. Add 2 tablespoons of the salt and return to a rolling boil. Blanch the ramp greens until wilted, about 20 seconds. Using a slotted spoon or spider, transfer the greens to a colander and run them under cold water. Drain and squeeze out the excess water.

2. Bring the water back to a boil. Add the pasta and cook until al dente according to package directions.

3. While the pasta cooks, prepare the pesto: In a food processor, combine the hazelnuts, ramp bulbs and stems, and 1 teaspoon kosher salt. Pulse together until roughly chopped.

4. Add the ramp greens, olive oil, and Pecorino Romano and pulse together until a paste forms. Drizzle in more oil if needed to obtain a silky consistency. Transfer the pesto to a large bowl.

5. Add ½ cup pasta water to the bowl to loosen the pesto. Add the cooked pasta directly to the bowl and toss to combine.

6. Plate in bowls and season with salt and pepper, if desired.

PASTA with 'NDUJA & SPRING VEGETABLES

I let the Hudson Farmers' Market be my guide for this pasta that combines spicy 'nduja, a spreadable salami, with peak spring vegetables and just a bit of cream. The vegetables are blanched until just cooked through so they maintain their snappy texture and sweet flavor, which cuts the richness of the sauce. **SERVES 4**

2 tablespoons kosher salt

¾ pound gemelli or fusilli

1 bunch asparagus, trimmed and cut on an angle into 1-inch pieces

½ pound sugar snap peas, ends trimmed and halved crosswise

3 tablespoons olive oil

1 cup frozen pearl onions

4 ounces 'nduja

½ cup heavy cream

2 tablespoons roughly chopped fresh tarragon

1. Bring a large pot of water to a boil. Add the salt and return to a rolling boil. Add the pasta and cook for 1 minute less than the package directions for al dente instruct. Add the asparagus and snap peas and cook until crisp and tender, 1 minute more.

2. While the pasta cooks, prepare the sauce: Heat the oil in a 12-inch skillet over medium heat. Add the pearl onions and sauté until they begin to brown in spots, about 5 minutes. Remove and set aside. Add the 'nduja to the skillet, breaking it up with the back of a spoon. Cook until it melts, about 2 minutes. Add the cream, bring to a simmer, and cook until the sauce begins to thicken, about 2 minutes.

3. Return the onions to the skillet and add the pasta and vegetables directly to the skillet. Toss to coat until the pasta becomes glossy, adding ¼ cup of pasta water or more (up to 1 cup), as needed to loosen up the sauce.

4. Plate in bowls and top with the tarragon.

> **COOK'S NOTE:** I like to use asparagus that's on the leaner side for this recipe as I find that fat stalks aren't as flavorful. However, you don't want them pencil thin. This recipe also calls for frozen pearl onions for ease. If you feel strongly about using fresh, keep in mind it will add extra time and preparation to the recipe as you'll need to trim their roots and boil them before peeling.

TOMATO "SALAD" PASTA

In New York, tomato season usually coincides with the hottest months of summer, so this recipe works well for many reasons. It's a good way to use all the candy-colored tomatoes you've hopefully accumulated, and you don't have to slave over a hot stove. All you need to do with ingredients this fresh is toss them with some grassy olive oil and fresh herbs and then let them hang out while you boil some water for pasta. **SERVES 4**

2 pints cherry, grape, or baby Sun Gold tomatoes, halved lengthwise

2 cloves garlic, finely chopped

½ teaspoon crushed red pepper flakes

¼ cup chopped flat-leaf Italian parsley, plus more for garnish

¼ cup torn basil leaves, plus more for garnish

2 tablespoons torn oregano leaves, plus more for garnish

¼ cup good-quality olive oil, plus more for drizzling

Kosher salt

Freshly ground black pepper

¾ pound short tubular pasta such as penne

¼ cup grated Pecorino Romano or Parmesan cheese, plus more for serving

1. In a large bowl, combine the tomatoes, garlic, red pepper flakes, herbs, and olive oil. Stir together gently to coat the ingredients and season with 1 teaspoon of salt and black pepper to taste. Cover and let sit at room temperature for 30 minutes, allowing the flavors to come together.

2. Bring a large pot of water to a boil. Add 2 tablespoons of the salt and return to a rolling boil. Add the pasta and cook until al dente according to package directions.

3. Add the pasta directly to the bowl of tomatoes and toss to coat. Stir in the Pecorino Romano and toss again.

4. Plate in bowls. Garnish with additional parsley, basil, and oregano. Season with salt and black pepper and drizzle with olive oil. Pass additional grated Pecorino Romano at the table, if desired.

COOK'S NOTE: I love using a mixture of different color tomatoes, such as gold and red and sometimes even green, for a brightly colored dish.

COOK'S NOTE: This recipe calls for slab bacon, which is primarily cut from the belly and does not come pre-sliced. This allows you to get a thicker dice than you would from grocery-store bacon, and gives you a texture that stands up to the toothsome pasta.

"BLT" PASTA

In the summer, I eat a tomato sandwich nearly every day. On some days it's simply toasted bread with mayonnaise and thickly cut tomatoes seasoned with big chunks of flaky Maldon salt and a few turns of fresh pepper. On others, Chad will fry up some bacon from a local farm in Kinderhook, New York, then stack the crispy slices atop tomatoes and bitter greens or farm-fresh lettuce for a sandwich that screams summer. I use watercress for this recipe because it wilts well but still maintains great crunch and texture. It also adds a nice savory note, balancing the sweetness of the tomatoes and the saltiness of the bacon. **SERVES 4**

Kosher salt

4 ounces slab bacon, cut into ½-inch dice (see Cook's Note)

1 tablespoon olive oil

¾ pound mezze rigatoni

1 pound cherry or baby Sun Gold tomatoes, halved (about 3 cups)

Freshly ground black pepper

5 ounces watercress, roughly chopped

Grated Pecorino Romano cheese, for serving

1. Bring a large pot of water to a boil. Add 2 tablespoons of the salt and return to a rolling boil.

2. While the water comes to a boil, prepare the sauce: Place the bacon and olive oil in a 12-inch skillet over medium-low heat. Cook until the bacon is crisp, stirring occasionally to make sure it does not burn, about 8 minutes. Remove the bacon and set aside. Pour off all but 2 tablespoons fat from the pan.

3. Add the pasta to the boiling water and cook until al dente according to package directions.

4. Add the tomatoes to the skillet and cook over medium heat, coating them in the bacon fat. Season with salt and pepper. As the moisture from the tomatoes releases and deglazes the pan, scrape up any browned bits on the bottom of the pan. Sauté the tomatoes until they are tender and almost melt, about 5 minutes more. Add half of the bacon to the skillet and toss together to combine.

5. Increase the heat to medium-high. Add the pasta directly to the skillet and toss to coat. Add the watercress and ½ cup pasta water and toss until the watercress wilts, adding ¼ cup more of pasta water (up to 1 cup), as needed to loosen up the sauce.

6. Plate in bowls, season with salt and pepper, and top with the remaining bacon. Pass the grated Pecorino Romano at the table.

ORECCHIETTE with FRESH CORN & BURRATA

The Hudson Farmers' Market overflows with corn in August. I'm always quick to pile more ears than needed into my tote to bring home for quick, fresh meals such as a corn soup (which I like to garnish with pickled chiles) or a simple corn salad tossed with herbs to accompany grilled fish. It also freezes beautifully for your winter chowder needs (just cut the corn off the cob before freezing). Because I'm buying the freshest, sweetest ears I can find I throw the kernels in raw, for a no-cook summer sauce. If needed, feel free to sauté the corn quickly in butter beforehand. This dish is made extra special with a topping of velvety burrata and a showering of fresh herbs. **SERVES 4**

Kosher salt

¾ pound orecchiette

4 ears corn

4 tablespoons unsalted butter, at room temperature

½ teaspoon crushed red pepper flakes

¼ cup sliced chives (cut on an angle into ½-inch lengths), plus more for garnish

¼ cup roughly chopped fresh mint, plus more for garnish

¼ cup torn basil leaves, plus more for garnish (see Cook's Note)

Freshly ground black pepper

1 ball burrata (about 8 ounces), torn into small chunks

Flaky salt, such as Maldon or Jacobsen (optional)

Grated Pecorino Romano cheese, for serving

1. Bring a large pot of water to a boil. Add 2 tablespoons of the kosher salt and return to a rolling boil. Add the pasta and cook until al dente according to package directions.

2. While the pasta cooks, prepare the sauce: Shuck the corn, but leave the stems attached. Wipe the corn with a kitchen towel to remove any silky strands. Stand an ear upright in a large bowl and use a chef's knife to carefully cut the kernels off into the bowl using a downward motion. Discard the cobs. Add the butter, red pepper flakes, chives, mint, and basil to the bowl and toss together gently. Season with salt and black pepper.

3. Add the pasta and ½ cup pasta water directly to the corn mixture, stirring to combine and melt the butter.

4. Plate in bowls, scatter the burrata on top, and garnish with additional herbs. Season with flaky salt and black pepper, if desired. Pass the grated Pecorino Romano at the table.

COOK'S NOTE: I like to chiffonade (cut into little ribbons) the basil to garnish this dish. This simple French technique makes a big impression. Simply stack the leaves on top of each other, roll them tightly into a cigar shape, and cut it crosswise into thin slices, which will unfurl to be elegant wisps.

PASTA with BACON, PEAS & LEEKS

When you feel you have nothing to cook, look to the season for inspiration. This spring-ish weeknight dish combines smoky bacon with sweet peas and leeks for a sophisticated supper in a snap. This recipe calls for bacon, but pancetta or prosciutto would work nicely as well, and if leeks are not on hand, shallots or onions are a fine substitute. **SERVES 4**

Kosher salt

¾ pound mezze rigatoni or other short tubular pasta

¼ pound bacon, cut into ½-inch pieces

2 medium leeks, white and light green parts only, halved lengthwise and thinly sliced crosswise

Freshly ground black pepper

1 cup fresh peas or 1 cup frozen baby peas

¼ cup chopped flat-leaf Italian parsley

¾ cup grated Grana Padano or Parmesan cheese

1. Bring a large pot of water to a boil. Add 2 tablespoons of the salt and return to a rolling boil. Add the pasta and cook until al dente according to package directions.

2. While the pasta cooks, prepare the sauce: Cook the bacon until crisp in a 12-inch skillet over medium heat, stirring often to make sure the bacon does not burn, about 4 minutes. Remove the bacon and set aside on a plate lined with paper towels.

3. Pour off all but 2 tablespoons of the bacon fat, add the leeks to the skillet, and sauté over medium-low heat until they are translucent, about 4 minutes. Season with salt and pepper.

4. Add the pasta and peas directly to the skillet and toss to coat. Increase the heat to medium-high, sprinkle in the bacon, and toss again, adding ¼ cup of pasta water or more (up to 1 cup), as needed to loosen up the sauce. Season with salt and pepper, if desired.

5. Plate in bowls and sprinkle with the parsley. Pass the grated cheese at the table.

SPAGHETTINI with SALSA VERDE

This herbaceous and briny pesto has lots of personality thanks to the combination of anchovies, capers, and lemon zest. If using oregano, it should take a backseat when combined with other herbs as it can be overpowering. This sauce also works served alongside grilled skirt steak or chicken with a squeeze of lemon juice as a zippy side. **SERVES 4**

Kosher salt

¾ pound spaghettini or other long, thin pasta

1 clove garlic, roughly chopped

2 cups roughly chopped mixed fresh herbs, such as parsley, mint, and oregano

3 anchovy fillets or 1 tablespoon anchovy paste

2 tablespoons capers, rinsed well if salt-packed

Zest of 1 lemon

½ cup olive oil

¼ cup grated Parmesan cheese

1. Bring a large pot of water to a boil. Add 2 tablespoons of the salt and return to a rolling boil. Add the pasta and cook until al dente according to package directions.

2. While the pasta cooks, prepare the pesto: In a food processor, combine the garlic, herbs, anchovies, capers, and half the lemon zest and pulse until they are coarsely chopped. Add the olive oil in a slow steady stream, pulsing until combined.

3. Pour the pesto into a large bowl and stir in the cheese.

4. Add the pasta directly to the pesto and toss to coat until the pasta becomes glossy, adding ¼ cup of pasta water or more (up to 1 cup), as needed to loosen up the sauce.

5. Plate in bowls and top with the remaining lemon zest.

PESTO ALLA TRAPANESE

Our friends Andrew and Michael have the most glorious farm-house and garden in Tivoli, New York. They grow row upon row of different tomato varietals along with just about every other vegetable under the sun. One summer while they were on vacation, they put us in charge of "picking" to ensure that their surplus of produce would go to good use. I was more than happy to oblige! This Sicilian-inspired pesto makes perfect use of midsummer's tomato rush and abundance of fresh herbs. This dish can be served warm or at room temperature.

SERVES 4

Kosher salt

¾ pound gemelli

¼ cup blanched whole almonds

1 pound cherry or grape tomatoes, preferably heirloom and halved if large

1 large clove garlic

2 cups roughly chopped mixed herbs, rinsed and patted dry, plus more for garnish (see Cook's Note)

½ teaspoon crushed red pepper flakes

½ cup olive oil

¼ cup grated Pecorino Romano cheese

Freshly ground black pepper

COOK'S NOTE: Nearly any mixed herbs will fit the bill for this recipe. I love using basil, mint, and parsley together, but sage, thyme, and/or rosemary would also be lovely.

1. Bring a large pot of water to a boil. Add 2 tablespoons of the salt and return to a rolling boil. Add the pasta and cook until al dente according to package directions.

2. While the pasta cooks, prepare the pesto: Toast the almonds in a 12-inch skillet over medium heat, stirring occasionally to make sure they do not burn, about 3 minutes. Remove and set aside.

3. In a food processor, combine the tomatoes, garlic, herbs, almonds, 1 teaspoon kosher salt, and the red pepper flakes and pulse gently until thoroughly combined. Pour the olive oil in a slow, steady stream into the food processor while pulsing so the mixture begins to emulsify. Continue until all of the oil has been combined and the sauce forms a smooth paste.

4. Transfer the mixture to a large bowl and fold in the Pecorino Romano. Season with additional salt and black pepper.

5. Add the pasta directly to the bowl with the pesto and toss until all of the strands are coated, adding ¼ cup of pasta water or more (up to 1 cup), as needed to loosen up the sauce.

6. Place in bowls and garnish with additional herbs.

SUMMER CORN & TOMATO PASTA

Nick and Sarah Suarez moved to the Hudson area right around the same time as Chad and I did. They had also relocated from Brooklyn, and dreams of opening their own restaurant landed them in Germantown. We watched as they put tireless hours of work into creating one of the most beautiful spaces I've seen. Their spot, Gaskins, is a Hudson Valley tavern, but it's so much more: a meeting place for all of our friends and the community where they welcome everyone with open arms. Nick served me this dish one night and I instantly fell in love with it. I've tweaked it ever so slightly, but you'll see it's the perfect combination of the valley's summer bounty. **SERVES 4**

4 ears corn

Kosher salt

¾ pound fettuccine

3 tablespoons olive oil

4 cloves garlic, thinly sliced

Freshly ground black pepper

¼ cup white wine

4 tablespoons butter

¼ cup grated Parmesan cheese, plus more for serving

1 pint mixed cherry or Sun Gold tomatoes, halved

2 tablespoon fresh lemon juice

1 bunch of sorrel, cut into a chiffonade (see Cook's Note on page 116)

1. Shuck the corn, leaving the stems attached. Wipe the corn with a kitchen towel to remove any silky strands. Stand the ear upright in a large bowl and use a chef's knife to carefully cut the kernels off the cob using a downward motion.

2. Bring a large pot of water to a boil. Add 2 tablespoons of the salt and return to a rolling boil. Add pasta and cook until al dente according to package directions.

3. While the pasta cooks, prepare the sauce: Heat the oil in a 12-inch skillet over medium heat. Add the garlic and sauté until pale golden, making sure it does not brown, about 2 minutes. Add the corn to the pan and cook until it begins to gently brown in spots, 5 to 7 minutes. Season with salt and pepper.

4. Increase the heat to high under the skillet and add the white wine, followed by 1 cup of the pasta water, and bring to a simmer. Scoop the pasta directly into the skillet along with the butter and Parmesan, stirring to coat. Cook until the sauce begins to emulsify, about 2 minutes, adding an additional ¼ cup of pasta water or more (up to 1 cup), if needed to loosen up the sauce.

5. Remove from the heat and add the cherry tomatoes, tossing again to coat the tomatoes. Add the lemon juice and toss again. Season with salt and pepper.

6. Plate in bowls and garnish with the sorrel and more Parmesan, if desired.

PASTA with SUMMER SQUASH, SARDINES & PRESERVED LEMON

One late summer night, our friends Gabby and Rachel had us over for supper. Not wanting to cut into our hang time, they quickly pulled together this supper utilizing the incredible amounts of zucchini the summer bumper crop brought upon us. The resulting recipe combines the mighty squash with tinned sardines, lots of fresh herbs, and, of course, fresh breadcrumbs made from a day-old loaf of bread from their Hudson bakery, Bonfiglio & Bread. I added some preserved lemon to give this dish a bright, funky lift. **SERVES 4**

BREADCRUMBS

1 tablespoon olive oil

½ cup fresh or panko breadcrumbs

Flaky salt, such as Maldon

PASTA AND SAUCE

Kosher salt

¾ pound gemelli or rotini

4 tablespoons olive oil, plus more for drizzling

2 cloves garlic, thinly sliced

½ teaspoon crushed red pepper flakes

1 tablespoon roughly chopped preserved lemon

6 baby yellow squash and green zucchini, julienned

½ cup chopped mixed fresh herbs, plus more for garnish

Freshly ground black pepper

Two 4-ounce cans oil-packed sardines, drained

1. **Prepare the breadcrumbs:** Heat the oil in a 12-inch skillet over low heat. Toast the breadcrumbs until golden, stirring occasionally, about 4 minutes. Remove from the heat, season with the flaky salt, and set aside.

2. **Cook the pasta:** Bring a large pot of water to a boil. Add 2 tablespoons of the kosher salt and return to a rolling boil. Add the pasta and cook until al dente according to package directions.

3. **While the pasta cooks, prepare the sauce:** Wipe out the skillet and heat the oil over medium heat. Add the garlic and cook until pale golden, about 2 minutes. Add the red pepper flakes and preserved lemon and cook 1 minute more. Add the squash and cook until crisp-tender, about 5 minutes. Stir in the herbs, cooking 1 minute more. Season with salt and black pepper.

4. Increase the heat to medium-high. Add the pasta directly to the skillet and toss to coat. Add the sardines, toss again to combine, and cook until they are just heated through, 1 minute more, adding ¼ cup of pasta water or more (up to 1 cup), as needed to loosen up the sauce.

5. Plate in bowls, top with the breadcrumbs, and garnish with fresh herbs. Drizzle with olive oil and season with salt and black pepper.

BELA LIGHTLY SMOKED PORTUGUESE
SARDINES IN OLIVE OIL

(U)

WILD CAUGHT - ALL NATURAL - PACKED FRESH

Net Weight 4-1/4 OZ (120g)

COOK'S NOTE: When cooking the eggplant, try to not disturb it too much so it evenly browns, which is key for the texture of this dish.

RIGATONI ALLA NORMA

For this dish, you crisp slick, deeply hued eggplants in hot oil and toss them with fresh tomato sauce seasoned with earthy oregano and hot pepper. With cooler nights and shorter days, making this pasta is a nice way to transition from summer to fall. I do not salt my eggplant first. This not only saves you time, but they get crispier this way, I promise. **SERVES 4**

5 tablespoons olive oil, plus more as needed

1 medium eggplant (about 1½ pounds), unpeeled, cut into 1-inch dice

1 teaspoon flaky salt, such as Maldon or Jacobsen

Kosher salt

¾ pound rigatoni

1 large shallot, finely chopped

1 tablespoon chopped fresh oregano, plus more for garnish

1 thinly sliced fresh red chile pepper, such as cayenne

One 28-ounce can diced San Marzano tomatoes

Freshly ground black pepper

¾ cup grated ricotta salata

¼ cup torn basil leaves

1. Bring a large pot of water to a boil.

2. While the water comes to a boil, heat 3 tablespoons of the oil in a 12-inch skillet over medium-high heat. Working in batches so as not to crowd the pan, add the eggplant and fry until golden brown, adding more oil if the eggplant looks like it's drying out. Eggplants tend to absorb a lot of moisture. Remove the eggplant, sprinkle with the flaky salt, and set aside.

3. Add 2 tablespoons of the kosher salt to the pot of boiling water and bring the water back to a rolling boil. Add the pasta and cook until al dente according to package directions.

4. While the pasta cooks, prepare the sauce: Wipe out the pan, then heat the remaining 2 tablespoons of olive oil in the skillet over medium heat. Add the shallot and cook until softened, 3 minutes. Add the oregano and chile pepper and cook 2 minutes more. Add the tomatoes and bring to a simmer. Season with kosher salt and black pepper.

5. Two minutes before the pasta is done cooking, add the eggplant back to the skillet and stir to coat. Add the pasta directly to the pan and toss together.

6. Plate the pasta in bowls and top with the ricotta salata, basil, and extra oregano.

STROZZAPRETI with BROCCOLINI, ANCHOVY & ALMONDS

This straightforward pasta dish relies heavily on greens and is layered with flavor. I love broccolini for its sweetness, and when coupled with salty anchovies and red pepper flakes, and topped with crunchy almonds, you'll see how this will quickly become part of your weeknight rotation. If you find cauliflower or broccoli are closer at hand, feel free to use them instead. **SERVES 4**

Kosher salt

2 bunches broccolini (about 1 pound), tough ends trimmed, cut into thirds

¾ pound strozzapreti or fusilli

½ cup chopped almonds

2 tablespoons olive oil

3 tablespoons butter

2 cloves garlic, thinly sliced

½ teaspoon crushed red pepper flakes

4 anchovy fillets or 1 tablespoon anchovy paste

¼ cup grated Pecorino Romano cheese, plus more for serving

Freshly ground black pepper

1. Bring a large pot of water to a boil. Set up a bowl of ice water nearby. Add 2 tablespoons of the salt to the boiling water and return to a rolling boil. Blanch the broccolini in the water for 2 minutes. Remove and place in the ice bath to stop it from cooking further. Bring the water back to a boil, add the pasta, and cook until al dente according to package directions.

2. While the pasta cooks, prepare the sauce: Toast the almonds in a 12-inch skillet over medium heat until they begin to brown, about 3 minutes. Remove and set aside.

3. Wipe the skillet clean and heat the oil and butter over medium-low heat. Add the garlic and red pepper flakes and sauté until the garlic is pale golden, about 2 minutes. Add the anchovies and stir until they melt, 1 minute more. Add a ½ cup of pasta water and simmer for 1 minute until sauce emulsifies. Add the broccolini and toss together to coat.

4. Scoop the pasta directly into the skillet and toss together with the broccolini, adding ¼ cup of pasta water or more (up to 1 cup), as needed to loosen up the sauce. Stir in the Pecorino Romano and toss again. Season with salt and black pepper.

5. Plate in bowls and sprinkle with the toasted almonds. Pass grated cheese at the table, if desired.

BONFIGLIO BUCATINI with MUSHROOMS, MINT & CHILI OIL

We had no kitchen in Hudson for about a year as we renovated, and we spent many weekend mornings at Bonfiglio & Bread enjoying perfectly executed pastries such as sticky buns, almond *kouign-amanns*, and *schnecken*. Always in favor of the savory option, my favorite breakfast was their mushroom toast served on house-made sourdough with chili oil and mint and topped with an egg. Once my kitchen was in order, I had to try this at home—but on pasta, *mais oui*. **SERVES 4**

2 tablespoons olive oil

4 tablespoons butter

1½ pounds mixed mushroom caps, such as cremini, shiitake, and oyster, sliced (if you can only find creminis, that's A-OK)

2 tablespoons roughly chopped fresh thyme

Kosher salt

Freshly ground black pepper

¾ pound bucatini or other long pasta

1 cup red wine

¼ cup chopped flat-leaf Italian parsley

4 large egg yolks, the freshest you can find (optional; see Cook's Note)

2 tablespoons fresh mint, torn, for garnish

Chili oil, for drizzling (store-bought or homemade; recipe follows)

1. Bring a large pot of water to a boil.

2. While the water comes to a boil, start the sauce: Heat the oil and 2 tablespoons of the butter in a 12-inch skillet over medium heat. Once the butter melts, add the mushrooms and thyme and sauté until they begin to cook down and become deeply browned, about 9 minutes. Season with salt and pepper.

3. Add 2 tablespoons of the salt to the boiling water and return to a rolling boil. Add the pasta to the boiling water and cook until al dente according to package directions.

4. While the pasta cooks, finish the sauce: Add the wine to the skillet and bring to a simmer. Cook until the liquid has nearly evaporated, about 5 minutes. Add the pasta directly to the skillet, stirring in the remaining 2 tablespoons butter and the parsley, tossing to combine until the butter melts and the sauce is glossy. Add in ¼ cup of pasta water or more (up to 1 cup), as needed to loosen up the sauce.

5. Quickly plate in bowls and gently place an egg yolk, if desired, on top of each dish. Garnish with the torn mint leaves and drizzle with the chili oil.

CHILI OIL MAKES 1 CUP

1 cup olive oil

1 tablespoon crushed red pepper flakes

1. Combine the olive oil and red pepper flakes in a small saucepan. Cook over low heat for about 4 minutes.

2. Remove from the heat and let cool to room temperature before using. Transfer to a sealed container and refrigerate for up to 1 month.

> COOK'S NOTE: Feel free to fry or poach an egg instead of using raw yolks. I recommend keeping the yolk runny to help bring the sauce together.

FARRO PASTA with "BLACK" TOMATO SAUCE

When I first started writing this cookbook, it became a big topic of conversation everywhere I went. Mostly because I was over-the-top excited, but also because people were eager to share their own back pocket pastas with me. This recipe comes straight from Rome and the pantry of designer Kevin Walz. He moved his daughters, Jersey and Addison, to Italy when they were young. Now living in Hudson, Jersey was kind enough to share her father's recipe with me. The "black" is a loose reference to the color the pasta and sauce take on after they are tossed with the basil and the walnuts. **SERVES 4**

3 tablespoons olive oil, plus more for drizzling

2 cloves garlic, thinly sliced

One 28-ounce can whole San Marzano tomatoes

Kosher salt

Freshly ground black pepper

¾ pound farro or whole wheat spaghetti

1 cup chopped walnuts

10 whole basil leaves, plus more for garnish

Grated Parmesan cheese, for serving

Flaky salt, such as Maldon or Jacobsen

1. Heat 1½ tablespoons of the olive oil over medium heat. Add the garlic and sauté until pale golden, about 2 minutes. Immediately add the tomatoes, breaking them up with the back of a spoon. Cook until they are soft, adding in a tablespoon or two of water if they seem to be drying out, about 20 minutes. Season with salt and pepper.

2. While the sauce simmers, cook the pasta: Bring a large pot of water to a boil. Add 2 tablespoons of the kosher salt and return to a rolling boil. Add the pasta and cook until al dente according to package directions.

3. While the pasta cooks, finish the sauce: Heat the remaining 1½ tablespoons olive oil in a second skillet over medium-high heat. Add the walnuts and toast, stirring constantly, until they start to brown evenly and smell like popcorn, about 5 minutes. Immediately stir the walnuts into the cooked tomatoes. Cook for another 5 minutes, then add the basil leaves. The sauce should darken to a deep, rich red.

4. Scoop the pasta directly into the skillet and toss to coat, adding ¼ cup of pasta water or more (up to 1 cup), as needed to loosen up the sauce.

5. Plate in bowls, drizzle with oil, and top with the grated Parmesan, flaky salt, and a few grinds of black pepper. Top with additional torn basil.

BRAISED HUNTER'S CHICKEN RAGU

Chicken thighs are an ideal ingredient in our house. They have more flavor than breast meat and are priced well to boot. I often roast them for chili and quick soups, or braise them in bunches, then play around with different flavors for meals all week long. This recipe is a take on chicken cacciatore, which is hearty winter fare. The nice thing about braises is that they can be made a day or two in advance, which only intensifies and betters their essence. Twenty minutes before you're ready to eat, just warm up the sauce while you pour yourself a glass of wine. **SERVES 4**

¼ cup dried porcini mushrooms (optional, but recommended)

1 medium carrot, roughly chopped

1 stalk celery, roughly chopped

1 large shallot, roughly chopped

3 cloves garlic

6 bone-in, skin-on chicken thighs (about 2 pounds)

Kosher salt

Freshly ground black pepper

2 tablespoons olive oil

½ teaspoon crushed red pepper flakes

1 tablespoon fresh rosemary, roughly chopped

1 tablespoon fresh thyme

¼ cup chopped flat-leaf Italian parsley, plus more for garnish

½ pound cremini mushrooms, quartered

1. If using the dried mushrooms, place them in a bowl and pour in 1 cup boiling water. Let sit 15 minutes to soften the mushrooms. Reserving ½ cup of the soaking liquid, drain the mushrooms through a paper towel. Roughly chop the mushrooms and set aside.

2. In a food processor, combine the carrot, celery, shallot, and garlic. Pulse together until minced. Set aside.

3. Season the chicken with salt and black pepper. Heat the oil in a 12-inch skillet over medium heat. Add the chicken skin side down first and brown well, about 5 minutes on each side. Remove and set aside.

4. Pour off all but 3 tablespoons of fat from the skillet. Add the vegetables to the skillet and cook until they soften and begin to brown, about 5 minutes. Add the red pepper flakes, rosemary, thyme, and half the parsley and cook together 2 minutes more. Add the fresh mushrooms and cook until they begin to soften, about 3 minutes. Stir in the tomato paste.

5. Add the wine and reserved mushroom liquid (if using) and bring to a simmer. Cook until the liquid has almost evaporated, about 2 minutes. Add the chicken stock and cook until the sauce has reduced by about half, about 5 minutes more. Stir in the tomatoes and porcinis. Season with salt and black pepper. Return the chicken to the skillet

1 tablespoon tomato paste

½ cup dry red wine, such as Pinot Noir or Cabernet

1 cup chicken stock, plus more for braising

One 28-ounce can whole or diced San Marzano tomatoes

¾ pound rigatoni or other tubular pasta

¼ cup grated Pecorino Romano cheese

and bring to a simmer, cooking for 30 minutes, adding more chicken stock if the chicken braise begins to dry out. Remove the chicken and when it's cool enough to touch, shred the meat, discard the skin and bones, and return the meat to the skillet.

6. While the sauce simmers, cook the pasta: Bring a large pot of water to a boil. Add 2 tablespoons of the salt and return to a rolling boil. Add the pasta and cook until al dente according to package directions.

7. Add the pasta directly to the skillet and toss to combine, adding ¼ cup of pasta water or more (up to 1 cup), as needed to loosen up the sauce.

8. Plate in bowls and top with the Pecorino Romano. Garnish with the remaining parsley.

Braised Hunter's Chicken Ragu, page 130

LEMONY SPAGHETTI

In Hudson, the winters are long and cold and sometimes it feels like the warmer months will never come. This bright, citrusy pasta perks up the doldrums that can set in and offers a nice break from the heavy braises and roasts that we usually turn to this time of year. If you can get your hands on some Meyer lemons, please use them. Their flavor is sweeter than a regular lemon and somewhat less acidic. I often keep heaps of citrus around, and when I plate the spaghetti I sometimes add grated orange or grapefruit zest on top for a pop of color and extra zip.

SERVES 4

3 lemons

Kosher salt

¾ pound spaghetti

1 tablespoon olive oil

2 tablespoons unsalted butter

½ cup heavy cream

1 cup grated Parmesan cheese, plus more for serving

5 ounces baby arugula

Freshly ground black pepper

1. Zest and juice the lemons and set them aside separately. You should have about 2 tablespoons of zest and ½ cup of juice.

2. Bring a large pot of water to a boil. Add 2 tablespoons of the salt and return to a rolling boil. Add the pasta and cook until al dente according to package directions.

3. When the pasta is about 5 minutes away from being al dente, heat the oil in a 12-inch skillet over medium heat. Add the butter and cook until melted, about 2 minutes. Add the cream and bring to a simmer, then add the lemon juice and half the zest and cook together for 2 minutes more or until slightly reduced.

4. Scoop the pasta directly into the skillet, stirring vigorously. Stir in ½ cup of pasta water along with the Parmesan and arugula. Toss to coat until the arugula wilts, adding ¼ cup of pasta water or more (up to 1 cup), if needed to loosen up the sauce.

5. Plate in bowls and garnish with the remaining lemon zest. Serve with Parmesan cheese and salt and pepper, if desired.

BAKED ZITI with CRÈME FRAÎCHE & SPINACH

Baked ziti is meant to feed a crowd, and this surely does. Ricotta cheese has a tendency to dry out when baked, so I split the difference with silky crème fraîche, which adds a slight tanginess to the pasta and lightens the texture just a bit. Chad always adds spinach when he's in charge of dinner, so I've included it here, too. Although this dish is unassuming enough for the middle of the week, I like to dig into this on a cold Sunday night—then you can look forward to leftovers for lunch the next day. **SERVES 6 TO 8**

1 cup ricotta cheese

1 cup crème fraîche

1 egg

1 cup grated Pecorino Romano cheese

Kosher salt and freshly ground black pepper

2 tablespoons olive oil

1 medium onion, chopped

2 cloves garlic, thinly sliced

1 teaspoon crushed red pepper flakes

1 tablespoon roughly chopped fresh oregano

1 pound sweet or spicy Italian sausage, casings removed

One 28-ounce can plus one 14-ounce can diced San Marzano tomatoes

1 pound ziti

5 ounces baby spinach

¾ pound mozzarella, cut into ½-inch pieces

1. In a large bowl, combine the ricotta, crème fraîche, egg, and ½ cup of the Pecorino Romano. Season with salt and black pepper and set aside.

2. Heat the oil in a 12-inch skillet over medium heat. Add the onion and cook until softened, about 4 minutes. Add the garlic, red pepper flakes, and oregano and cook for 2 minutes more. Add the sausage and cook until browned, breaking up the meat with the back of a wooden spoon. Add the tomatoes and bring to a simmer. Season to taste and cook until the sauce has thickened, about 20 minutes.

3. Preheat the oven to 400°F.

4. Bring a large pot of water to a boil. Add 2 tablespoons of the salt and return to a rolling boil. Add the pasta and cook for 4 minutes short of al dente according to package directions. Drain, reserving ½ cup pasta water.

5. Add the spinach to the sauce with ½ cup pasta water, stirring until it wilts. Remove from the heat. Stir half of the sauce into the ricotta mixture. Add the pasta and toss together to coat. Pour the pasta into a 13 x 9-inch baking dish. Top with the remaining sauce. Sprinkle the mozzarella and remaining ½ cup Pecorino Romano over the top and bake until the cheese starts bubbling, about 20 minutes.

6. Set the oven to broil and broil until the cheese and pasta are browned in spots, about 5 minutes more. Remove from the oven and let rest for 5 minutes before serving.

PAPPARDELLE with DUCK CONFIT, OLIVES & RAISINS

One fall I made more duck confit legs than I knew what to do with—I'm talking pounds and pounds of duck. To this day, I'm not quite sure what I was thinking, but I do know that my house smelled really good for many days and I had plenty of meat on my hands for making this delicious pasta dish. This recipe calls for store-bought confit, which is a huge timesaver for this special occasion meal. **SERVES 4**

4 store-bought duck confit legs (see Cook's Note), at room temperature

¼ cup golden raisins

1 small yellow onion, chopped

1 medium carrot, chopped

1 celery stalk, chopped

2 cloves garlic

Kosher salt

¾ pound pappardelle

2 tablespoons olive oil

1 tablespoon roughly chopped fresh thyme

1 tablespoon roughly chopped fresh rosemary

1 cup green olives, pitted and halved

Freshly ground black pepper

½ cup dry white wine

1 cup chicken stock

¼ cup grated Parmesan, plus more for serving

¼ cup roughly chopped flat-leaf Italian parsley

1. Pull the meat off the duck legs and shred (discard the skin and bones). Soak the raisins in warm water for 10 minutes, then drain and set aside.

2. In a food processor, combine the onion, carrot, celery, and garlic. Pulse together until minced.

3. Bring a large pot of water to a boil. Add 2 tablespoons of the salt and return to a rolling boil. Add the pasta and cook until al dente according to package directions.

4. While the pasta cooks, prepare the sauce: Heat the oil in a 12-inch skillet over medium heat. Add the vegetable mixture and cook until softened, about 4 minutes. Stir in the thyme and rosemary. Add the duck meat, raisins, and olives and stir together, cooking 1 minute more. Season with salt and pepper.

5. Add the wine, bring to a simmer, and cook until the liquid has almost evaporated, about 2 minutes. Add the chicken stock and cook until the sauce has reduced by half, about 5 minutes, adding a small amount of pasta water if the sauce starts to dry out.

6. Add the pasta directly to the skillet and toss to coat, adding ¼ cup pasta water or more (up to 1 cup), as needed to loosen up the sauce. Add the cheese and toss again.

7. Plate in bowls and garnish with the parsley. Pass grated cheese at the table.

COOK'S NOTE: Duck confit legs are available at most gourmet food stores or can readily be purchased online.

PORCHETTA PASTA

You can turn anything into a hearty pasta dish with leftover meat. Roast pork shoulder, pot roast, coq au vin all work well here—it's really just a matter of using up the protein you have on hand. Not all of us are lucky enough to have Mona Talbott's porchetta readily available, but if you're coming up this way, it's worth stopping at Talbott & Arding (and grabbing enough for your back pocket pasta). Or seek porchetta out at your local Italian butcher. While we waited for the construction on our house to finish, I found myself itching to make dinner with no kitchen to cook in. Our kind neighbors Roger and Brad allowed this pasta princess to cook for them at their place one Sunday evening, and into the sauce went our extra porchetta. **SERVES 4**

Kosher salt

¾ pound short tubular pasta

2 tablespoons olive oil

1 small onion, finely chopped

1 pound porchetta or cooked roast, cut into ½-inch dice

½ cup red wine

One 28-ounce can diced San Marzano tomatoes

¼ cup chopped flat-leaf Italian parsley

Freshly ground black pepper

Grated Pecorino Romano cheese, for serving

1. Bring a large pot of water to a boil. Add 2 tablespoons of the salt and return to a rolling boil. Add the pasta and cook until al dente.

2. While the pasta cooks, prepare the sauce: Heat the oil in a 12-inch skillet over medium heat. Add the onion and cook until softened, about 4 minutes. Add the porchetta and cook 3 minutes more.

3. Pour in the wine and deglaze the pan, scraping up the browned bits on the bottom of the pan. Stir in the tomatoes and half of the parsley. Fill the tomato can halfway with water, swish it around, and add the water to the pan. Season with salt and pepper. Allow the sauce to simmer for 12 minutes.

4. Add the pasta directly to the skillet and toss to coat, adding ¼ cup pasta water or more (up to 1 cup), as needed to loosen up the sauce.

5. Plate in bowls and top with the remaining parsley. Pass the Pecorino Romano at the table.

BROWN BUTTERED SQUASH BAKE

Looking for an indulgent supper? Combine salty, nutty brown butter with sage and Fontina, then add some sweet roasted butternut squash. When the weather starts to dip, this is your welcome-to-fall plate of goodness, which I've served many times while entertaining at home in Hudson. It also transports easily, for those days when you're potlucking on the go. **SERVES 6**

1 medium butternut squash (about 2½ pounds)

2 tablespoons olive oil

2 tablespoons plus 1 teaspoon kosher salt, plus more to taste

Freshly ground black pepper

¾ pound large shell pasta

3 tablespoons unsalted butter

1 bunch (about 20 leaves) fresh sage, chopped, plus more for garnish

1¾ cups crème fraîche

½ pound Fontina cheese, shredded

⅛ teaspoon freshly grated nutmeg

Flaky salt, such as Maldon or Jacobsen (optional)

1. Preheat the oven to 450°F.

2. Peel the squash, then halve lengthwise, scrape out the seeds, and cut into 1-inch pieces. Add to a large bowl, toss with the olive oil and 1 teaspoon of the kosher salt, and season with pepper.

3. Arrange the squash in a single layer on a rimmed baking sheet. Roast until the squash is golden in color and begins to caramelize, 30 to 35 minutes. Remove from the oven and set aside in a large bowl.

4. Bring a large pot of water to a boil. Add 2 tablespoons of the kosher salt and return to a rolling bowl. Add the pasta and cook until al dente according to package directions.

5. While the pasta cooks, melt the butter in a saucepan over medium heat and cook until the butter begins to foam, turns golden in color, and smells nutty, about 2 minutes. Add the sage leaves and remove from the heat. Pour the brown butter over the squash. Add the crème fraîche and half of the Fontina to the squash and gently toss together. Season with the nutmeg and kosher salt and pepper and toss again.

6. When the pasta is done, drain and add to the bowl with the squash mixture. Toss together.

7. Pour the mixture into a 13 x 9-inch baking pan. Top with the rest of the Fontina and bake until the pasta is bubbling and the cheese is melted, about 20 minutes. Remove from the oven and let stand for 5 minutes before serving. Garnish with additional sage leaves and a sprinkling of flaky salt.

SPELT PASTA with SAUSAGE, GREENS & WALNUT GREMOLATA

Every January I try (somewhat unsuccessfully) to hit the reset button, hence the spelt pasta, which is high in fiber and has a more toothsome texture than regular durum wheat. I make this with spicy pork sausage, but if you want to go even cleaner, swap in turkey or chicken sausage, which will also work nicely. Same with the greens and nuts. Swiss chard, mustard greens, almonds, or hazelnuts would be great substitutions. **SERVES 4**

GREMOLATA

⅓ cup roughly chopped walnuts

1 tablespoon lemon zest

¼ cup roughly chopped flat-leaf Italian parsley

Flaky salt, such as Maldon

PASTA AND SAUCE

Kosher salt

¾ pound short tubular spelt pasta

4 tablespoons olive oil

1 pound hot Italian sausage, casings removed

½ cup white wine or dry vermouth

2 cloves garlic, minced

1 large bunch Tuscan kale or other sturdy greens, tough stems removed, leaves cut into ½-inch-wide ribbons

Freshly ground black pepper

Grated Pecorino Romano cheese, for serving

1. **Make the gremolata:** Toast the walnuts in a 12-inch skillet over medium heat until golden, about 4 minutes. Remove and let cool. Wipe the skillet clean. Toss the walnuts with the lemon zest and parsley and season with flaky salt. Set aside.

2. **Prepare the pasta:** Bring a large pot of water to a boil. Add 2 tablespoons of the kosher salt and return to a rolling boil. Add the pasta and cook until al dente according to package directions.

3. **While the pasta cooks, prepare the sauce:** Heat 2 tablespoons of the oil in the skillet over medium heat. Add the sausage and cook until browned, breaking up the meat with the back of a wooden spoon, about 10 minutes. Remove and set aside. Pour the drippings over the sausage.

4. Increase the heat under the skillet to high and add the white wine to deglaze, scraping up the browned bits from the bottom of the pan. Pour over the sausage.

5. Reduce the heat to medium and heat the remaining 2 tablespoons oil in the skillet. Add the garlic and cook until pale golden, about 2 minutes. Begin adding the kale to the pan by the handful, cooking until it wilts. Add ½ cup pasta water to help it along. Return the sausage to the pan and stir together. Season with salt and pepper.

6. Add the pasta to the skillet, tossing to coat, adding ¼ cup pasta water or more, as needed to loosen up the sauce. Plate in bowls and top with the gremolata and Pecorino.

travels
near & far

on the road at home

POBLANO CHILE RISOTTO

In Distrito Federal, or "DF," my friend Nils, who knows Mexico City like his backyard, showed us the ins and outs of the city's street food and fine dining, including where to get the crispiest carnitas, and, of course, he helped us drink all of the mezcal we could handle. Over a late lunch at Sud 777 we had a dish called Arroz Cremoso de Chile Poblano—and you know where my mind went. Nils helped me translate it to a pasta dish and this is the result: simple, spicy, and satisfying, and also a nice option for vegetarians. **SERVES 4**

3 large or 4 medium poblano chile peppers

½ teaspoon kosher salt, plus more to taste

2 packed cups roughly chopped greens such as kale, chard, collards, or turnip greens

4 cups vegetable or chicken stock

Freshly ground black pepper

4 tablespoons olive oil

½ large yellow onion, diced

1 cup Arborio rice

2 tablespoons Mexican *crema* or sour cream, plus more for serving

1. Roast the poblanos directly over a gas flame or under a broiler, until soft and blackened all over. Place in a bowl, cover with plastic wrap, and set aside for 15 minutes to steam.

2. Under cool running water, rub off the charred skins (it's okay if some charred bits remain) and remove the stems, seeds, and ribs. Place the chiles and ½ teaspoon of the salt in a food processor and pulse until the mixture is a coarse purée. Set aside.

3. Combine the greens and stock in a large saucepan and bring to a boil. Let the greens simmer until tender, about 15 minutes. Reserving the liquid, drain the greens well and set aside. Return the reserved stock to the saucepan and bring to a simmer. Season with salt and pepper.

4. Meanwhile, heat 2 tablespoons of the olive oil in a 12-inch skillet over medium heat. Add the onion and cook until translucent, about 4 minutes. Add the remaining 2 tablespoons olive oil and the rice and stir until the rice turns chalky in color, about 2 minutes.

5. Begin adding the hot stock about ¼ cup at a time, stirring constantly and allowing the rice to absorb the liquid before adding more stock, about 15 minutes total. When you've

used about two-thirds of the hot stock, stir the poblano purée into the rice and continue adding the remaining stock, stirring constantly, until the rice is tender but still toothsome, about 10 minutes more. If the rice is still tough and you've run out of stock, feel free to use water, cooking the rice until it is done.

6. Add the greens to the rice with a little splash of water, if necessary, to avoid burning the rice; heat until the greens are warmed through. Stir in the *crema* and season with salt and pepper.

7. Plate in bowls and top with extra *crema*, if desired.

PASTA with FAVAS & PEAS

The year we traveled to Mexico City it was the end of March, when the cold weather in New York City had not yet disappeared and the green-market was still bleak. The warm sun and friendly vibes were just what we needed. We wandered the streets eating some of the best street food I've ever had. On one corner a woman was serving *tlacoyos*, a blue corn masa cake topped with fava beans and queso fresco. They were heavenly—a promise that spring was on the way. **SERVES 4**

1 cup ricotta cheese

1 cup pea shoots, cut into thirds

Zest of 1 lemon

¼ cup roughly chopped mint leaves, plus more for garnish

½ cup grated Pecorino Romano cheese, plus more for serving

Kosher salt

Freshly ground black pepper

¾ pound creste di gallo pasta or farfalle

2 tablespoons olive oil

¼ pound pancetta, cut into ½-inch pieces

1 cup frozen fava beans, thawed

1 cup fresh or frozen baby peas, thawed if using frozen

1. In a large bowl, combine the ricotta, pea shoots, lemon zest, mint, and Pecorino Romano. Season with salt and pepper. Set aside.

2. Bring a large pot of water to a boil. Add 2 tablespoons of the salt and return to a rolling boil. Add the pasta and cook until al dente according to package directions.

3. While the pasta cooks, prepare the sauce: Heat the oil in a 12-inch skillet over medium heat. Add the pancetta and cook until crispy, about 5 minutes. Remove and set aside.

4. Add the fava beans and peas to the skillet and heat through, about 2 minutes. Toss in the pancetta. Add the pasta directly to the skillet and toss together to coat.

5. Stir the pasta mixture into the ricotta, adding ¼ cup of pasta water or more (up to 1 cup), as needed to loosen up the sauce.

6. Plate in bowls and garnish with mint. Season with salt and pepper, if desired. Pass Pecorino Romano at the table.

LINGUINE with ASPARAGUS & LEMON

Good traveling companions are hard to find, so when you do meet them, hold on to them tight. One summer, we went to Ischia off the coast of Naples, Italy, with our frequent flying partner Anna Dunne. We shared a house with a friend of Anna's named Martha and her friend Ned as well as our other girlfriends Sarah and Lizzie. We all became fast friends and, months later, Martha had us over to her apartment in New York for a reunion dinner where she cooked us the only thing that made sense: pasta, of course. **SERVES 4**

Kosher salt

¾ pound linguine

1 bunch asparagus, trimmed and cut on an angle into 1-inch pieces

2 tablespoons olive oil

3 tablespoons unsalted butter

Zest and juice of 2 lemons

1 cup grated Parmesan cheese, plus more for serving

Freshly ground black pepper

¼ cup chopped flat-leaf Italian parsley

1. Bring a large pot of water to a boil. Add 2 tablespoons of the salt and return to a rolling boil. Add the pasta and when the pasta is just 2 minutes short of al dente (according to package directions), add the asparagus and cook until crisp-tender. Drain the pasta and asparagus and reserve 2 cups of the pasta water.

2. While the pasta and asparagus cook, prepare the sauce: Heat the oil in a 12-inch skillet over medium heat. Add the butter and cook until melted, about 2 minutes. Add the lemon zest and juice and cook together until slightly reduced, about 1 minute more. Add in 1 cup of the pasta water and cook until the sauce emulsifies, about 1 minute.

3. Add the pasta and asparagus and toss vigorously to coat. Add the Parmesan and stir again. Season with salt and pepper.

4. Plate in a large bowl and sprinkle with the parsley. Pass Parmesan at the table.

SPAGHETTI ALLA FORIANA

This recipe hails from our trip to the island of Ischia. It's traditionally served there during Lent, with nuts that stand in for meat, which many Catholics give up during this time. With its dramatic cliffs, aqua sea, and warm welcomes, Ischia quickly became home, if even for just a little while. We also discovered the Falanghina grape variety while visiting, which makes for an expressive, citrusy white wine with minerality; it's produced in the Campania region. We drank copious amounts of it while there. My friend Jordan Salcito produces one called "Caldera" under her Bellus label, and it would pair beautifully with this.

SERVES 4

3 cloves garlic

½ cup pine nuts

½ cup walnuts

Kosher salt

¾ pound spaghetti

3 tablespoons olive oil

1 tablespoon chopped fresh oregano

Freshly ground black pepper

½ cup golden raisins

4 tablespoons butter

¼ cup chopped flat-leaf Italian parsley

1. In a food processor, combine the garlic, pine nuts, and walnuts and pulse together until finely chopped.

2. Bring a large pot of water to a boil. Add 2 tablespoons of the salt and return to a rolling boil. Add the pasta and cook until al dente according to package directions.

3. While the pasta cooks, prepare the sauce: Heat the olive oil in a 12-inch skillet over medium-high heat. Add the nut and garlic mixture to the pan, stir in the oregano, and season with salt and pepper. Cook for 3 minutes. Add the raisins and cook 1 minute more.

4. Add the pasta directly to the skillet and toss to coat. Add the butter and toss again until the butter melts and the sauce is glossy, adding ¼ cup of pasta water or more (up to 1 cup), as needed to loosen up the sauce.

5. Plate in bowls and season with salt and pepper, if desired. Garnish with the parsley.

BONNIE SLOTNICK'S PASTA with SPINACH & GOAT CHEESE

I had the pleasure of interviewing legendary cookbook collector and shop owner Bonnie Slotnick for *Cherry Bombe* magazine. Over the course of the conversation I had to ask what quick pasta recipe she relied upon. Bonnie is a lifetime New Yorker and like most of us who live here, she understands that kitchen space is at a premium. This is Bonnie's no-fuss, one-pot recipe that she goes back to time and time again. Her only requirement is that you buy the freshest ingredients available, preferably at the farmers' market. **SERVES 4**

Kosher salt

¾ pound fettuccine or other long, thin pasta

4 ounces fresh goat cheese (the freshest you can find), crumbled

10 ounces baby spinach

Freshly ground black pepper

Zest and juice of 1 lemon (optional)

1. Bring a large pot of water to a boil. Add 2 tablespoons of the salt and return to a rolling boil. Add the pasta and cook until al dente according to package directions. Reserving the pasta water, drain the pasta.

2. Return the pasta to the pot and heat over medium-low heat. Immediately add the goat cheese and ½ cup of the pasta water to the pasta, stirring until the cheese melts. Add the spinach and an additional ½ cup of pasta water and continue to stir until the spinach wilts. Add ¼ cup of pasta water or more (up to 1 cup), as needed to loosen up the sauce. Season with salt and pepper and stir in the lemon zest and juice, if using.

3. Serve the pasta directly from the pot.

CARAMELIZED FENNEL & HAZELNUT PASTA

Caramelizing fennel makes all the difference, so make sure you take the time to do so for this Roman-inspired dish. Sometimes, I'll even cook double the amount of fennel called for and use the remainder throughout the week—tossing it into salads or serving it as a side warmed and topped with crumbled goat cheese. **SERVES 4**

1 large fennel bulb

Kosher salt

¾ cup hazelnuts

3 tablespoons olive oil

½ teaspoon crushed red pepper flakes

¾ pound linguine fini or other long, thin pasta

3 cups chopped tomatoes (about 3 medium)

Freshly ground black pepper

½ cup grated Pecorino Romano cheese, plus more for serving

¼ cup chopped flat-leaf Italian parsley

1. Core the fennel bulb and thinly slice it lengthwise. Roughly chop 3 tablespoons of the fronds and set aside.

2. Bring a large pot of water to a boil. Add 2 tablespoons of the salt and return to a rolling boil.

3. Meanwhile, toast the hazelnuts in a 12-inch skillet over medium heat until golden, about 4 minutes. Wrap the nuts in a kitchen towel and rub vigorously to remove the skins (it's fine if they all do not come off). Chop the hazelnuts (should yield about ½ cup) and set aside.

4. Wipe out the pan and heat the olive oil over medium heat. Add the sliced fennel and cook until it softens and begins to caramelize, about 13 minutes. Add the red pepper flakes and cook 1 minute more.

5. Toss the pasta into the boiling water and cook until al dente according to package directions.

6. Meanwhile, add the tomatoes to the skillet and season with salt and pepper. Cook until they begin to break down, about 5 minutes.

7. Increase the heat to medium-high. Add the pasta directly to the skillet and toss until the sauce evenly coats the pasta, adding ¼ cup of pasta water or more (up to 1 cup), as needed to loosen up the sauce. Stir in the Pecorino Romano and half of the parsley and toss again.

8. Plate in bowls and season with salt and black pepper. Top with the toasted hazelnuts, remaining parsley, and reserved fennel fronds. Pass Pecorino Romano at the table, if desired.

GRILLED SQUID with CHILES & MINT

My love for seafood runs deep, and this recipe combines quickly grilled squid tossed with lemon, chiles, and mint for a dish that's best served by the seashore or on a weeknight when you want to pretend you're on vacation. You must also drink white wine with this, preferably very chilled—and lots of it. **SERVES 4**

⅓ cup plus 2 tablespoons olive oil, plus more for drizzling

Zest and juice of 2 lemons

2 to 3 serrano chile peppers, thinly sliced

3 scallions, white and green parts, cut into ½-inch pieces, plus more for serving

½ cup roughly chopped mint leaves, plus more for serving

Kosher salt

Freshly ground black pepper

¾ pound linguine

1 pound squid, cleaned (see Cook's Note) and patted very dry

Flaky salt, such as Maldon or Jacobsen

1. Heat the grill or grill pan to high.

2. In a large bowl, combine ⅓ cup of the olive oil, the lemon zest and juice, chiles, scallions, and mint. Toss everything together and season with salt and black pepper.

3. Bring a large pot of water to a boil. Add 2 tablespoons of the kosher salt and return to a rolling boil. Add the pasta and cook until al dente according to package directions.

4. While the pasta cooks, grill the squid: Season the squid with salt and pepper and the remaining 2 tablespoons oil and grill over high heat, about 2 minutes on each side. You want a good char, but you don't want to overcook the squid or the meat will turn rubbery.

5. Remove the squid from the heat and cut into ¼-inch-thick slices. Add to the bowl with the olive oil and herbs. Toss everything together.

6. Add the pasta directly to the squid and toss to coat. Add ¼ cup of pasta water or more (up to 1 cup), as needed to loosen up the sauce. Season with salt and pepper.

7. Plate in a large bowl. Drizzle with oil and garnish with additional mint and scallions. Garnish with the flaky salt.

> **COOK'S NOTE:** Squid is generally sold cleaned, but confirm with your fishmonger just to make sure. Given the option, I would spend the few extra dollars to buy it as such. It can be a messy business. Also, make sure to pat your squid very dry before grilling to ensure you get good grill marks.

FIDEOS with COCKLES & CHORIZO

Chad and I took a life-changing trip with our friends Talia, Ashley, and Jacque to Cádiz, Spain. For one week straight we did nothing but drink sherry (still do—can't stop, won't stop) and eat cured meats and everything imaginable straight from the ocean. There is something magical about the brininess of cockles coupled with the smokiness of the chorizo, and it always takes me back to that special time and place. *Fideos* is Spain's equivalent of pasta and I've adapted this traditional Catalan recipe, which the incredibly talented Anthony Sasso, who is the chef at Casa Mono, Manhattan's best Spanish restaurant, shared with me. **SERVES 4**

SHERRY AIOLI

1 very fresh egg yolk, at room temperature

1 clove garlic, minced

¼ teaspoon kosher salt, plus more to taste

1 tablespoon sherry vinegar

½ cup canola oil or other neutral oil

FIDEOS

¾ pound cappellini

2 tablespoons olive oil

6 ounces Spanish chorizo, cut into ½-inch dice

2 cloves garlic, thinly sliced

16 cockles

4 cups chicken stock

Juice of ½ a lemon

1. **Make the sherry aioli:** In a metal bowl, whisk together the egg yolk, garlic, salt, pepper, and sherry vinegar. In a steady stream, pour in the oil slowly, whisking constantly until it thickens and emulsifies. Season with more salt if needed. Set aside.

2. Preheat the oven to 300°F.

3. Working in batches, wrap about ¼ pound of pasta in a kitchen towel and snap the long pieces into tiny 1-inch pieces by breaking the noodles in half several times.

4. Lay the pasta in a thin layer on a large rimmed baking sheet, exposing as much of the pasta to the heat of the oven as possible. Toast the pasta for about 30 minutes, checking every few minutes to make sure that the noodles are toasting evenly, shaking the pan as necessary to ensure they do not burn. Remove from the oven and set aside. Set the oven to broil.

5. Heat the oil, chorizo, and garlic in a large ovenproof low-sided pan over medium heat. Cook until the chorizo renders its fat and the garlic turns golden, about 4 minutes. Add the pasta and cockles to the skillet. Pour in enough stock to submerge the pasta, about 4 cups. Increase the heat to high and cook until the stock has evaporated and the cockles have opened, about 3 minutes.

6. Place the pan under the broiler and broil until the noodles start to curl and toast at the edges, 3 to 5 minutes. Remove and season with the lemon juice. Serve with sherry aioli.

FETTUCCINE with CRAB & JALAPEÑOS

One June I was invited to Decatur Island in the San Juans off the coast of Washington State. I was with one of my oldest friends, Suzy, and her family and we cooked the whole weekend at her parents' house, which overlooks the Pacific. Her father, Art, made a version of this sauce, and I fell in love with its brightness and the heat from the jalapeños. I've been putting my take on it ever since. Here, I use Dungeness crab, which the region is known for, but feel free to use blue or lump if you can't find Dungeness. **SERVES 4**

Kosher salt

¾ pound linguine

2 tablespoons olive oil

3 small shallots, thinly sliced

2 medium jalapeño chile peppers, thinly sliced

4 tablespoons unsalted butter

½ teaspoon crushed red pepper flakes

Zest and juice of 3 lemons

Freshly ground black pepper

¾ pound cooked, shelled fresh Dungeness crab, picked over for bits of shell

3 scallions (white and light green parts only), thinly sliced

1. Bring a large pot of water to a boil. Add 2 tablespoons of the salt and return to a rolling boil. Add the pasta and cook until al dente according to package directions.

2. While the pasta cooks, prepare the sauce: Heat the oil in a 12-inch skillet over medium heat. Add the shallots and jalapeños and cook until they both begin to crisp and turn golden, about 5 minutes. Remove the shallot mixture from the skillet and set aside.

3. Wipe out the pan, add 2 tablespoons of the butter and the red pepper flakes and cook over medium heat until the butter is melted, about 1 minute. Add half of the lemon zest and all of the lemon juice and cook 1 minute more. Season with salt and black pepper.

4. Increase the heat under the skillet to medium-high. Add the crab and 1 cup of pasta water and bring to a simmer. Add the pasta directly to the skillet and add the remaining 2 tablespoons butter, tossing until the butter melts and the sauce becomes glossy, adding ¼ cup of pasta water or more (up to 1 cup), as needed to loosen up the sauce.

5. Plate the pasta in bowls and garnish with the scallions, fried shallots and jalapeños, and remaining lemon zest.

CAMPANELLE with BROCCOLI RABE & CHORIZO

I adore broccoli rabe for its long stems, assertive greens, and petite buds. This recipe calls for blanching the broccoli rabe while the pasta cooks to help bite off some of its bitterness. I swapped in smoky, garlicky Spanish chorizo in place of the more traditional Italian sausage, but, as always, use what you've got. **SERVES 4**

Kosher salt

¾ pound campanelle

1 bunch broccoli rabe, cut into 1-inch pieces, tough ends discarded

2 tablespoons olive oil

2 cloves garlic, thinly sliced

½ pound Spanish chorizo, cut into ½-inch dice

¼ cup grated Pecorino Romano cheese

1. Bring a large pot of water to a boil. Add 2 tablespoons of the salt and return to a rolling boil. Add the pasta, and 2 minutes before it's al dente according to package directions, add the broccoli rabe and cook until crisp-tender.

2. While the pasta cooks, prepare the sauce: Heat the olive oil in a 12-inch skillet over medium heat. Add the garlic and cook until pale golden, about 2 minutes. Remove the garlic from the skillet and set aside.

3. Add the chorizo to the pan and cook until crisp, about 4 minutes.

4. Add the garlic, pasta, and broccoli rabe directly to the skillet with the chorizo and toss to combine, adding ¼ cup of pasta water or more (up to 1 cup), as needed to loosen up the sauce. Stir in the Pecorino Romano and toss again. Plate in bowls.

This page: Vineyards on
the outskirts of Lago di
Garda (Lake Garda), which
sits between Venice and
Milan

Previous page: The streets
of neaby Modena

TAGLIATELLE with OLIVES, ARUGULA & CARAMELIZED LEMONS

Long ribbons of noodles tangle with wilted arugula, oil-cured olives, and lemon for a bright and briny meal. I love to caramelize the lemons for some texture and crunch. I know you'll want to, but don't skip blanching the lemon slices before putting them in the oven; it helps to reduce bitterness, plus it takes only a few minutes. You've got this! **SERVES 4**

CARAMELIZED LEMONS

1 lemon, thinly sliced into rounds, seeds removed

1 tablespoon olive oil

½ teaspoon kosher salt

PASTA

2 tablespoons kosher salt

¾ pound tagliatelle

¼ cup olive oil

2 cloves garlic, thinly sliced

1 teaspoon crushed red pepper flakes

1 cup oil-cured black olives, pitted and roughly chopped

10 ounces baby arugula

¼ cup grated Pecorino Romano cheese, plus more for serving

Freshly ground black pepper

1. **Caramelize the lemons:** Preheat the oven to 325°F. Line a baking sheet with parchment paper.

2. Bring a medium saucepan of water to a boil. Add the lemon slices and cook for 2 minutes. Drain and pat dry.

3. Toss the lemons gently with the olive oil and season with the salt. Arrange the lemons in a single layer on the lined baking sheet. Roast until they begin to brown around the edges, about 25 minutes. Remove from the oven and set the lemons aside.

4. **While the lemons roast, cook the pasta:** Bring a large pot of water to a boil. Add the salt and return to a rolling boil. Add the pasta and cook until al dente according to package directions.

5. **While the pasta cooks, prepare the sauce:** Heat the oil in a 12-inch skillet over medium heat. Add the garlic and red pepper flakes and cook until the garlic is pale golden, about 2 minutes. Add the olives and cook 1 minute more.

6. Add the pasta directly to the skillet along with the arugula and Pecorino Romano. Stir in a ½ cup of pasta water and toss until the arugula wilts, adding an additional ¼ cup of pasta water or more (up to 1 cup), if needed to loosen up the sauce. Season with salt and pepper.

7. Plate in bowls and top with the caramelized lemon slices. Pass Pecorino Romano at the table, if desired.

MEZZE RIGATONI
with CHICKPEAS & PANCETTA

When you're craving soup but want something a bit more substantial, try translating your ingredients into pasta. This one, a take on Tuscan bean soup, involves warming chickpeas in pancetta fat with lots of herbs, then tossing the sauce with mezze rigatoni. Serve (as always) with a big glass of red wine, preferably Nebbiolo, which is a light- to medium-bodied wine with dried fruit and savory notes and little grip. Look for wines from the Lombardy and Langhe regions, which are more affordable than their sister bottles from Barbaresco and Barolo. **SERVES 4**

1 medium onion, quartered

1 medium carrot, roughly chopped

1 stalk celery, roughly chopped

3 cloves garlic, roughly chopped

½ cup flat-leaf Italian parsley leaves and stems

½ teaspoon crushed red pepper flakes

2 tablespoons olive oil, plus more for drizzling

¼ pound pancetta, cut into ½-inch pieces

Kosher salt

Freshly ground black pepper

1 tablespoon chopped fresh rosemary

1 tablespoon chopped fresh sage

¾ pound mezze rigatoni

2 tablespoons tomato paste

1. In a food processor, pulse the onion, carrot, celery, garlic, parsley, and red pepper flakes until minced. Transfer to a bowl and set aside.

2. Heat 1 tablespoon of the oil in a 12-inch skillet over medium-high heat. Add the pancetta and cook until crispy, about 4 minutes. Remove the pancetta from the skillet and set aside, reserving the fat in the pan.

3. Bring a large pot of water to a boil. Add 2 tablespoons of the salt and return to a rolling boil.

4. While the water comes to a boil, heat the remaining 1 tablespoon oil in the skillet over medium heat. Add the vegetable mixture and season with salt and black pepper. Cook and stir often until the vegetables begin to turn golden, about 9 minutes. Return the pancetta to the pan, add the rosemary and sage, and cook 1 minute more.

5. Add the pasta to the boiling water and cook until al dente according to package directions.

6. Meanwhile, stir the tomato paste into the sauce until combined. Add 1 cup of pasta water and bring the sauce to a simmer. Reduce the heat to low and cook until most of the liquid has evaporated, about 8 minutes. Stir in the chickpeas and cook 2 minutes more.

Two 15-ounce cans
chickpeas, drained and
rinsed

Grated Pecorino Romano
or Parmesan cheese, for
serving

7. Scoop the pasta directly into the skillet and toss to coat.
Add ¼ cup of pasta water or more (up to 1 cup), as needed
to loosen up the sauce. Season with salt and black pepper.

8. Plate in bowls and pass the grated cheese at the table.
Drizzle with olive oil, if desired.

COOK'S NOTE: If you have leftover greens lying
about, feel free to toss them in with the hot pasta at
the end to wilt them.

SAUSAGE RISOTTO with BALSAMIC-ROASTED SHALLOTS

Our East Williamsburg neighborhood is gentrifying at an alarming pace, and the news of our dear neighbors Jenn and Steve moving to Park Slope with their baby Brynn saddened me. It represented a change in my life that I wasn't expecting. Chad and I went to visit them in their new home, their boxes still unopened and a feeling of unsettledness in the air—one we all know too well after a big move. We told them to order a pizza—it wasn't the food that mattered, but our time together. However, Jenn, being Jenn, insisted on cooking for us, and with ease she pulled together a simple meal of sausage risotto served alongside balsamic-roasted red onions, which inspired me to create a similar dish at home. **SERVES 6**

SHALLOTS

4 small to medium shallots, unpeeled (see Cook's Note)

2 tablespoons olive oil

1 tablespoon good-quality balsamic vinegar

1 teaspoon light brown sugar

1 teaspoon kosher salt

1. **Make the shallots:** Preheat the oven to 425°F.

2. Trim the tops of the unpeeled shallots, then halve them through the root end.

3. In a large bowl, stir together the olive oil, balsamic vinegar, brown sugar, and salt. Add the shallots to the bowl and gently toss to coat. Place the shallots in a small, shallow baking pan and pour the rest of the balsamic mixture over the top.

4. Roast the shallots until tender, about 25 minutes, stirring the shallots halfway through the roasting time. Remove and set aside.

5. **Prepare the risotto:** Heat 2 tablespoons of the oil in a deep 12-inch skillet over medium-high heat. Add the sausage and cook until browned, breaking up the meat with the back of a wooden spoon, about 10 minutes. Remove the sausage from the skillet and set aside. Wipe the skillet.

6. Bring the chicken stock to a simmer in a large saucepan.

RISOTTO

4 tablespoons olive oil

1 pound hot Italian sausage, casings removed

8 cups chicken stock, preferably homemade

1 small yellow onion, minced

2 cups Arborio rice

½ cup dry white wine

1 cup grated Parmesan or Grana Padano cheese

2 tablespoons unsalted butter

Kosher salt and freshly ground black pepper

¼ cup roughly chopped flat-leaf Italian parsley

2 tablespoons roughly chopped fresh sage

7. Add the remaining 2 tablespoons olive oil to the skillet and heat over medium heat. Add the onion and cook until translucent, about 4 minutes. Add the rice and stir until it turns chalky in color and begins to smell toasted, about 2 minutes. Add the wine and cook until it evaporates, about 1 minute.

8. Begin adding the hot stock about ½ cup at a time, allowing the rice to absorb the stock before adding more, stirring constantly. Continue adding the stock by the ½ cup, stirring until all the liquid is absorbed and the rice is creamy in texture but is still al dente, 15 to 20 minutes.

9. Reduce the heat to low and fold in the sausage, cheese, and butter, tossing together until the butter has melted. Season with salt and pepper.

10. Plate in bowls and top with the parsley and sage. Serve with the balsamic-roasted shallots on the side.

COOK'S NOTE: I prefer to serve these shallots with their skins on for a pretty color contrast and crispy texture. If that's not your thing, the shallots easily slip out of their skins once roasted.

Sausage Risotto with Balsamic-
Roasted Shallots, page 182

SPAGHETTI AGLIO E OLIO with SAGE

Garlic, oil, cheese, repeat—honestly, dinner couldn't get simpler. The classic recipe of garlic and oil is perfectly fine on its own, but sage and hot pepper flakes give it a welcomed earthiness with a little kick. Pair this dish with a bottle of Montinore Pinot Noir as recommended by Rudy Marchesi, patriarch of Montinore Estate. **SERVES 4**

Kosher salt

¾ pound spaghetti

¼ cup olive oil

6 cloves garlic, thinly sliced

½ teaspoon crushed red pepper flakes

10 chopped sage leaves

¾ cup grated Pecorino Romano cheese, plus more for serving

½ cup chopped flat-leaf Italian parsley

Freshly ground black pepper

1. Bring a large pot of water to a boil. Add 2 tablespoons of the salt and return to a rolling boil. Add the pasta and cook until al dente according to package directions.

2. While the pasta cooks, prepare the sauce: Heat the olive oil in a 12-inch skillet over medium heat. Add the garlic and cook until golden, about 2 minutes, but make sure it does not brown. Add the red pepper flakes and sage and cook for 1 minute more. Add ½ cup of pasta water to the skillet and simmer until it reduces by half, about 2 minutes.

3. Reduce the heat to low and add the pasta directly to the skillet, tossing to coat. Add the Pecorino Romano and parsley and toss again to melt the cheese, adding ¼ cup of pasta water or more (up to 1 cup), as needed to loosen up the sauce. Season with salt and black pepper.

4. Plate in bowls and pass additional grated cheese at the table.

BUCATINI ALL'AMATRICIANA-ISH

This Roman dish generally calls for guanciale (cured pig jowl), but I like to use pancetta, which is more readily available and can be found at most grocery stores. If you can't find it, bacon works, too, but will give the sauce a smokier flavor (I've used it in the past with great results). I also opt for red onions as opposed to the yellow variety. Their sweetness couples nicely with this spicy, salty sauce, plus their pink color strewn throughout the sauce makes for vibrant contrast. **SERVES 4**

Kosher salt

¾ pound bucatini

1 tablespoon olive oil

¼ pound pancetta, cut into ½-inch dice

1 small red onion, thinly sliced

2 cloves garlic, thinly sliced

½ teaspoon crushed red pepper flakes

One 28-ounce can whole San Marzano tomatoes

Freshly ground black pepper

½ cup chopped flat-leaf Italian parsley

½ cup grated Pecorino Romano cheese, plus more for serving

1. Bring a large pot of water to a boil. Add 2 tablespoons of the salt and return to a rolling boil. Add the pasta and cook until al dente according to package directions.

2. While the pasta cooks, prepare the sauce: Heat the oil in a 12-inch skillet over medium heat. Add the pancetta and cook until crisp, about 5 minutes. Remove and set aside on a plate lined with a paper towel. Add the onion and cook until it begins to brown, about 5 minutes. Add the garlic and red pepper flakes and cook 2 minutes more.

3. Add the tomatoes to the skillet, crush them with a spatula or the back of a spoon, and stir to combine. Season with salt and black pepper and allow it to simmer while the pasta finishes cooking.

4. Add the pasta and parsley directly to the skillet and toss to combine, adding ¼ cup of pasta water or more (up to 1 cup), as needed to loosen up the sauce. Add the Pecorino Romano and toss again.

5. Plate in bowls and pass Pecorino Romano at the table, if desired.

PASTA with SHRIMP IN TOMATO CREAM

I met Suzy in 1999, when I moved to New York after college and she had just relocated from Portland, Oregon. We ended up as roommates in Brooklyn, and it was in that apartment in Fort Greene that we discovered the joys of cooking together on Sundays. Suzy's mom, Sally, passed this recipe down to her and, in turn, Suzy taught it to me. We still make it together to this day, nearly twenty years later. **SERVES 4**

Kosher salt

¾ pound fusilli

2 tablespoons olive oil

1 pound shrimp, peeled and deveined

Freshly ground black pepper

3 scallions, thinly sliced (dark green portion kept separate)

3 cloves garlic, thinly sliced

1 cup heavy cream

½ cup chicken stock

½ cup dry vermouth

½ cup dry-packed sun-dried tomatoes, thinly sliced

1 tablespoon tomato paste

1 cup crumbled feta cheese

¼ cup chopped flat-leaf Italian parsley

¼ cup fresh basil chiffonade (see Cook's Note, page 116)

1. Bring a large pot of water to a boil. Add 2 tablespoons of the salt and return to a rolling boil. Add the pasta and cook until al dente according to package directions.

2. While the pasta cooks, prepare the sauce: Heat the oil in a 12-inch skillet over medium-high heat. Season the shrimp with salt and pepper, add to the pan, and sauté until just cooked through, about 2 minutes. Remove and set aside in a large bowl.

3. Add the white and light green slices of scallions (reserve the dark green slices for garnish) and garlic to the pan and cook until softened, about 2 minutes. Remove and set aside in the bowl with the shrimp and cover.

4. Reduce the heat to medium. Stir in the cream, chicken stock, vermouth, sun-dried tomatoes, and tomato paste. Bring the sauce to a boil and simmer until the liquid has thickened and reduced by half, about 5 minutes. Return the shrimp mixture to the skillet and cook until heated through, about 2 minutes more.

5. Increase the heat to medium-high and add the pasta directly to the skillet, along with the feta, parsley, and half the basil. Toss everything together until the cheese begins to melt and the pasta is glossy with sauce. Season with salt and pepper.

6. Plate in bowls and garnish with the remaining basil and the scallion greens.

PASTA ALLA GRICIA

The combination of guanciale (cured pig jowl), salty Pecorino Romano, and black pepper brought together with some splashes of starchy pasta water is just what you'll want on a cold night. This is very similar to carbonara, but without the egg. If you can find guanciale, I highly recommend it, but pancetta will work in a pinch. **SERVES 4**

2 tablespoons kosher salt

¾ pound rigatoni or other large tubular pasta

1 tablespoon olive oil

6 ounces guanciale, cut into ½-inch dice

2 teaspoons freshly ground black pepper, plus more for serving

¾ cup grated Pecorino Romano cheese

1. Bring a large pot of water to a boil. Add the salt and return to a rolling boil. Add the pasta and cook it to just shy of al dente according to package directions.

2. While the pasta cooks, prepare the sauce: Heat the oil in a 12-inch skillet over medium heat. Add the guanciale and increase the heat to medium-high, cooking until the guanciale begins to brown and crisp, about 5 minutes. Remove and set aside.

3. Reduce the heat to medium. Add 1 cup of the pasta water to the skillet and simmer until the sauce has emulsified, about 2 minutes.

4. Add the pasta directly to the sauce, tossing vigorously to coat the pasta. Increase the heat to medium-high and add the guanciale, black pepper, and Pecorino Romano and toss again. The pasta is ready when it's slick with melted cheese and rendered pork fat.

5. Plate in bowls with additional black pepper, if desired.

COOK'S NOTE: Look for guanciale at gourmet Italian grocery stores such as Eataly or online at Zingerman's.

LINGUINE ALLE VONGOLE

I love saying the word *vongole*. Von-go-lay. There is something lyrical about the way it rolls off the tongue. Also, in terms of favorites, pasta with clams is pretty high up on my list. I've prepared this dish seaside on the Cape with clams I've dug up by hand. I also order it with wild abandon anytime I can, both stateside and abroad. **SERVES 4**

Kosher salt

¾ pound linguine

2 tablespoons olive oil

2 tablespoons unsalted butter

3 cloves garlic, thinly sliced

½ teaspoon crushed red pepper flakes, plus more for serving

½ cup white wine or dry vermouth

3 pounds littleneck clams, scrubbed (see Cook's Note)

½ cup roughly chopped flat-leaf Italian parsley, plus more for garnish

Freshly ground black pepper

1. Bring a large pot of water to a boil. Add 2 tablespoons of the salt and return to a rolling boil. Add the pasta and cook until al dente according to package directions.

2. While pasta cooks, prepare the sauce: Heat the oil and butter in a 12-inch skillet over medium-low heat. Add the garlic and red pepper flakes and cook until the garlic is pale golden, about 2 minutes. Add the wine, increase the heat to high, and bring to a boil. Add the clams and cover the skillet. Steam the clams until they open, about 5 minutes.

3. Transfer the cooked clams to a large bowl (discarding any that have not opened). Add the pasta directly to the skillet. Stir in the parsley and toss to coat. Add the clams and any accumulated juices to the skillet and toss again, adding ¼ cup of pasta water or more (up to 1 cup), as needed to loosen up the sauce. Season with salt and black pepper.

4. Plate in bowls with the clams on top. Add parsley for garnish and serve with red pepper flakes, if desired.

COOK'S NOTE: Making this recipe with fresh clams is a treat for sure, but when you just need that briny, buttery high and you're in a bind, canned clams work just fine. Just swap in two 6-ounce cans of chopped clams.

SPAGHETTI CARBONARA

Carbonara is my hangover food. Eggs, pork, pasta, and cheese? Come on! I would bet that you probably have some version of these ingredients in your fridge right now, which means you don't even need to leave the house (thank God). Make this when you have a wine headache and want to watch reruns of *Who's the Boss?* curled up on your couch while twirling noodles in a bowl. I like to finish mine with lots of freshly ground black pepper and extra cheese. **SERVES 4**

Kosher salt

¾ pound spaghetti

2 tablespoons olive oil

¼ pound pancetta, cut into ½-inch dice

3 eggs plus 1 egg yolk

¾ cup grated Pecorino Romano cheese, plus more for serving

Freshly ground black pepper

¼ cup chopped flat-leaf Italian parsley

1. Bring a large pot of water to a boil. Add 2 tablespoons of the salt and return to a rolling boil. Add the pasta and cook until al dente according to package directions.

2. While the pasta cooks, prepare the sauce: Heat the olive oil in a 12-inch skillet over medium heat. Add the pancetta and cook until crisp, about 5 minutes.

3. Meanwhile, in a large bowl, whisk together the whole eggs, egg yolk, Pecorino Romano, and salt and pepper to taste. Set aside.

4. With the skillet over medium heat, add the pasta directly to the skillet with ½ cup of pasta water, tossing together to combine.

5. Remove the pan from heat and add the egg mixture to the pan, tossing everything together quickly to ensure the egg doesn't scramble, until the pasta is glossy with sauce.

6. Plate in bowls and sprinkle with the parsley. Top with lots of additional cheese and pepper.

PASTA with MUSSELS & PECORINO ROMANO

The summer I went to Rome, I had the pleasure of meeting ex-pat Katie Parla, the coauthor of *Tasting Rome,* who lives in the Eternal City and provides food and art tours all over town. She was not only kind enough to show us around, but she also invited us to dinner with her family, who happened to be visiting, too. We dined at the incredible restaurant Trattoria da Cesare al Casaletto, where she pretty much ordered the whole menu for the table, including a pasta dish with mussels and plenty of Pecorino Romano. Generally, folks I've encountered have an issue with combining shellfish and grated cheese, but it has always spoken to me, and I rejoiced. Katie told me, "You learn the rules of Italian cooking to break them." I wholeheartedly agree. This dish is a nod in that direction. **SERVES 4**

¼ cup olive oil

1 pint cherry or grape tomatoes

4 cloves garlic, crushed with the side of a knife

1 shallot, finely chopped

1 teaspoon crushed red pepper flakes

Kosher salt

Freshly ground black pepper

¾ pound linguine or other long, thin pasta

2 pounds mussels, scrubbed clean and beards removed

1 cup white wine or dry vermouth

¾ cup grated Pecorino Romano, plus more for serving

¼ cup chopped flat-leaf Italian parsley

1. Bring a large pot of water to a boil.

2. Meanwhile, prepare the sauce: Heat the oil in a 12-inch skillet over medium-low heat. Add the tomatoes and cook until they begin to soften and burst, about 9 minutes.

3. Add the garlic and shallot to the tomatoes and cook until they begin to soften, about 4 minutes. Add the red pepper flakes and cook 1 minute more. Season with salt and black pepper.

4. Add 2 tablespoons of the salt to the boiling water and return to a rolling boil. Add the pasta and cook until al dente according to package directions.

5. While the pasta cooks, finish the sauce: Increase the heat under the skillet to medium-high and add the mussels and wine. Bring to a simmer, cover, and cook until the mussels open, about 3 minutes.

6. Remove the mussels from the pan (discarding any that have not opened) and set aside. Add the pasta directly to the skillet and toss to coat, adding ¼ cup of pasta water or more (up to 1 cup), as needed to loosen up the sauce. Stir in the Pecorino Romano. Return the mussels to the pan and toss to combine. Serve with the parsley and more cheese.

MOROCCAN LAMB RAGU

My trip to Marrakech was intense and overwhelming. The sights, smells, and sounds were sensory overload. Crimson reds, burnt oranges, and cerulean blues filled our days. We wandered the bustling market, ate from stalls at the Jemaa el-Fnaa, and got lost many, many times; it was an exploration and test of wills like none other. This recipe brings back memories of the flavors we experienced and the time spent in this mysterious place. **SERVES 4**

1 medium carrot, roughly chopped

2 medium shallots, roughly chopped

3 cloves garlic

2 tablespoons olive oil, plus more for drizzling

1 pound ground lamb

1 teaspoon ground coriander

1 teaspoon ground cumin

1 teaspoon ground cinnamon

1 teaspoon cayenne pepper

Kosher salt and freshly ground black pepper

1 tablespoon tomato paste

½ cup red wine

1 cup chicken stock or water

One 28-ounce can diced San Marzano tomatoes

¼ cup chopped flat-leaf Italian parsley

¾ pound fusilli lunghi

Greek yogurt, for serving

Torn mint leaves, for serving

Flaky salt, such as Maldon

1. Bring a large pot of water to a boil.

2. While the water comes to a boil, in a food processor, combine the carrot, shallots, and garlic. Pulse together until minced.

3. Heat the oil in a 12-inch skillet over medium heat. Add the vegetables and cook until they soften and begin to brown, about 5 minutes. Add the lamb and cook until browned, breaking up the meat with the back of a wooden spoon, about 6 minutes. Stir in the coriander, cumin, cinnamon, and cayenne. Season with kosher salt and black pepper. Stir in the tomato paste.

4. Add the wine and bring to a simmer. Cook until the liquid has almost evaporated, about 2 minutes. Add the chicken stock and cook until almost all the liquid has cooked down, about 5 minutes more.

5. Add the tomatoes and parsley, stir together, bring to a simmer, and let simmer while the pasta cooks (see Cook's Note).

6. Add 2 tablespoons of the kosher salt to the boiling water and return to a rolling boil. Add the pasta and cook until al dente according to package directions.

7. Add the pasta directly to the skillet and toss to coat with the sauce, adding ¼ cup of pasta water or more (up to 1 cup), as needed to loosen up the sauce.

8. Plate in bowls and top with a spoonful of yogurt, torn mint leaves, a drizzle of olive oil, and some flaky salt.

COOK'S NOTE: If the sauce seems like it needs more liquid while simmering, feel free to add small cups of pasta water to the pan during cooking. You want the sauce to be thick but to still have some movement.

salads
& sides

CHAD'S GARLIC BREAD

Chad makes the best garlic bread, hands down. So when he offers, I never say no. For this old-school recipe, he makes a soft compound butter with sautéed garlic and spreads it along both sides of the bread. Moments before the bread is done, he sets it under the broiler for a few minutes so that it gets extra crispy. **SERVES 6 TO 8**

1 baguette, split lengthwise

6 tablespoons unsalted butter, at room temperature

5 cloves garlic, finely chopped

2 tablespoons grated Pecorino Romano or Parmesan cheese

¼ cup chopped flat-leaf Italian parsley

1. Preheat the oven to 350°F. Line a baking sheet with foil.

2. Melt 2 tablespoons of the butter in a saucepan over medium heat. Add the garlic and cook until light golden, about 2 minutes. Pour the garlicky butter into a small bowl and allow it to cool. Once the melted butter has cooled, fold the mixture into the remaining softened butter.

3. Place the bread open-faced on the lined baking sheet. Spread the butter mixture over both slices of the baguette. Sprinkle with the cheese.

4. Bake until the bread begins to brown, about 12 minutes. Set the oven to broil and broil until the bread gets deep golden in color, 2 minutes more, checking frequently to make sure the bread does not burn. Remove from the oven, sprinkle with the parsley, and cut into 1-inch pieces to serve.

ESCAROLE SALAD with RED ONION, WALNUTS & APPLE

This salad features the best flavors of fall. Simply toss crunchy toasted walnuts, tart apple slices, and sturdy, bitter greens in a dressing made of sherry vinegar and spicy mustard. **SERVES 4**

1 cup chopped walnuts

1 large head escarole

1 apple, such as Cortland or Gala, halved, cored, and thinly sliced

¾ cup thinly sliced red onion

Kosher salt and freshly ground black pepper

Sherry Vinaigrette (recipe follows)

1. Toast the walnuts in a 12-inch skillet over medium heat, about 3 minutes. Remove from the skillet and set aside.

2. Discard the dark green leaves of the escarole and trim off the ends. Tear the remaining leaves into bite-size pieces.

3. In a large bowl, combine the toasted walnuts, escarole, apple, and onion. Season with salt and pepper and toss to combine. Dress the salad with sherry vinaigrette and toss again until the salad is evenly coated to your liking.

SHERRY VINAIGRETTE MAKES ABOUT ½ CUP

3 tablespoons good-quality sherry vinegar

1 teaspoon Dijon mustard

¼ cup olive oil

Kosher salt and freshly ground black pepper

1. In a large bowl, mix together the sherry vinegar and Dijon mustard.

2. Add the oil in a steady stream, whisking constantly until it emulsifies. Season with salt and pepper. The dressing will keep in a tightly sealed container in the refrigerator for up to 1 week.

SAUTÉED HEIRLOOM SUMMER BEANS

My friend Laura Ferrara and her husband, Fabio, own the beautiful Westwind Orchard in Accord, New York. It's a very special place. In addition to having a farm and selling organic apples, they also cook pizzas to order from a wood-fired oven Napoletano-style. I visited Laura one hot August day, and as I was leaving she started piling produce in my bag. Among her gifts were garlic, beautiful fresh and crinkly cayenne peppers, and stunning flat Romano beans. As she shooed me away like an Italian mama, she gave me very simple directions: Sauté the garlic and the peppers and then add the beans. I did exactly as she instructed. **SERVES 4**

3 tablespoons olive oil

3 cloves garlic, crushed with the side of a knife

2 cayenne chile peppers, thinly sliced

1 pound Romano or other green beans, trimmed (see Cook's Note)

Flaky salt, such as Maldon or Jacobsen, and freshly ground black pepper

1. Heat the oil in a 12-inch skillet over medium-high heat. Add the garlic and chiles and cook until the garlic begins to turn pale golden and the oil is fragrant, about 3 minutes. Remove the garlic and chiles and set aside.

2. Add the beans to the pan and sauté until they turn bright green and are crisp-tender, about 5 minutes. Reduce the heat to medium. Return the garlic and chiles to the skillet and toss to combine. Season with flaky salt and black pepper.

3. Plate on a large platter, family-style.

COOK'S NOTE: Find the freshest, most beautiful beans you can find at the farm stand. Look for different colors and shapes.

GRILLED PUNTARELLE with LEMON-ANCHOVY DRESSING

If you can find puntarelle—long, lean, and luscious greens—at the market, I highly recommend you bring a bunch home. I'm lucky that Sparrowbush Farm right outside of Hudson has such beauties close by. Escarole or another bitter green works, too, and taste just as great, but there is something incredibly elegant and sexy about the way these guys move. Plate them on a large platter for an impressive presentation. Even better? Pass the platter and eat them with your fingers.

SERVES 4

1 clove garlic, minced

1 teaspoon salt

3 anchovy fillets

Juice of 1 lemon

¼ cup olive oil, plus more for grilling

Kosher salt and freshly ground black pepper

1 bunch puntarelle

Flaky salt, such as Maldon or Jacobsen

1. Combine the garlic, salt, and anchovies in a mortar and use the pestle to smash together to create a paste. Add the lemon juice and stir to combine. Slowly whisk in the ¼ cup oil until the dressing emulsifies. Season with kosher salt and pepper.

2. Heat the grill to high. Drizzle the puntarelle with olive oil and season with kosher salt and pepper. Grill the greens over high heat, just long enough to get a good char, about 1 minute per side.

3. Plate the greens on a large platter and drizzle them with the dressing. Sprinkle with flaky salt.

COOK'S NOTE: Turn leftovers into a back pocket pasta by tossing hot pasta like linguine with the greens. A little pasta water goes a long way in creating a sauce, and if you have breadcrumbs, toast them up and place them on top before serving. Don't forget the grated Pecorino Romano, *per favore*.

CITRUS & FENNEL SALAD with ROSE WATER

Sweet, sour, and floral all at once, this vividly colored salad is a perfect pick-me-up for East Coast winter months. I typically serve this after a hearty and rich ragu pasta or one with a cream-based sauce. I've also put it out at brunch alongside a frittata that I made with leftover roasted vegetables. **SERVES 4**

1 large fennel bulb

2 blood oranges

1 navel orange

1 red or pink grapefruit

Kosher salt

2 tablespoons olive oil

1 tablespoon fresh lemon juice

1 teaspoon rose water (see Cook's Note)

1 teaspoon agave syrup

½ cup chopped roasted pistachios

Flaky salt, such as Maldon or Jacobsen

1. Halve and core the fennel bulb; reserve stalks for another use. Chop 2 tablespoons of the fronds and set aside. Using a mandoline, thinly slice the fennel and place in a large bowl.

2. Cut off the tops and bottoms of the oranges and use a paring knife to remove the peel, all of the pith, and the membrane. Cut the flesh crosswise into rounds. Repeat with the grapefruit and place all the citrus in the bowl with the fennel. Season with kosher salt.

3. In a small bowl, whisk together the olive oil, lemon juice, rose water, and agave.

4. Plate the citrus and fennel on a large platter and drizzle with the dressing. Top with the pistachios and chopped fennel fronds. Sprinkle with flaky salt.

COOK'S NOTE: I prefer the Al Wadi brand from Lebanon, which you can buy online at Kalustyan's, an incredible specialty food store in New York City. If you're ever visiting, it's worth a stop in to wander its labyrinth of a spice aisle.

GARLICKY BROCCOLI SALAD

This super simple salad has been in my family for as long as I can remember. It works as a refreshing side with just about everything and makes an appearance at almost every holiday. If you're worried about the raw garlic (I'm not!), add the garlic to the lemon juice about 15 minutes before-hand so it can mellow out a bit. **SERVES 4**

3 large lemons

2 cloves garlic, crushed through a garlic press

Kosher salt

1 medium head broccoli, cut into 3-inch spears, stalks and leaves removed

¼ cup olive oil

Flaky salt, such as Maldon or Jacobsen

1. Zest and juice the lemons (you should end up with ¼ cup of juice). Set aside the zest. In a small bowl, stir together the lemon juice and garlic.

2. Prepare a bowl of ice water. Fill a deep 12-inch skillet with water about two-thirds of the way up, so it will cover the broccoli when added. Bring the water to a boil. Salt the water, add the broccoli, and return to a rolling boil. Cook until crisp-tender, about 2 minutes. Remove and plunge the broccoli into the ice bath to stop it from cooking.

3. Remove the broccoli from the ice water and pat dry. Arrange it on a large plate or platter. Spoon the lemon juice and garlic mixture over the broccoli and drizzle with the oil. Sprinkle the lemon zest over the salad and add flaky salt to taste.

CARAMELIZED SUMMER TOMATOES

These beautifully plump, juicy, and intensely flavored tomatoes are a dream to bite into. You might also want to throw in a few ounces of crumbled ricotta salata or feta for some earthy oomph. Equally good? Serving these with soft scrambled eggs or piling them atop toasted bread. **SERVES 4**

2 pounds (about 2½ pints) red, gold, and orange cherry tomatoes, preferably heirloom, halved lengthwise

¼ cup olive oil

2 tablespoons chopped fresh oregano (thyme or rosemary will also work well)

2 teaspoons kosher salt, plus more to taste

1 teaspoon crushed red pepper flakes

1. Preheat the oven to 500°F. Line two rimmed baking sheets with parchment paper.

2. In a large bowl, combine the tomatoes, olive oil, oregano, salt, and red pepper flakes and stir together.

3. Place the tomatoes cut-side down on the baking sheet and bake until the tomatoes caramelize and the skins are shriveled but still juicy, about 10 minutes. Use immediately, store in the fridge for up to 1 week, or freeze for up to 3 months (see Cook's Note).

COOK'S NOTE: Cherry Tomatoes: To enjoy this dish all year round, double your batch and freeze them. Then, simply pop them out into a saucepan and cook over low heat, adding a splash of water if needed. I often use them for a quick *shakshuka* (baked eggs with tomatoes and harissa) or toss them with hot pasta and fresh herbs for supper.

CROUTONLESS CAESAR

I forgo the croutons in this salad because I usually serve it alongside pasta, but by all means add them back if you want. The salty, rich dressing is a welcome burst of brightness, especially when served alongside heavier dishes. This salad would work great alongside Quick Sausage Sugo (page 84), Smoky Garganelli alla Vodka (page 101), or Linguine alle Vongole (page 195). **SERVES 4**

1 clove garlic, minced

½ teaspoon kosher salt

4 anchovy fillets or
1 tablespoon anchovy paste

Juice of 1 lemon (about
2 tablespoons)

1 egg yolk, at room
temperature

½ cup grapeseed or
canola oil

¼ cup grated Pecorino
Romano or Parmesan
cheese, plus more for
serving

2 romaine hearts, torn into
bite-size pieces

Freshly ground black pepper

1. In a large nonreactive bowl mix together the garlic, salt, and anchovies to create a paste. Stir in the lemon juice and egg yolk. In a steady stream, add the oil, whisking constantly so the dressing emulsifies. Mix in the cheese.

2. Add the romaine leaves and toss to combine. Season with pepper. Top with more cheese, if desired.

Croutonless Caesar, page 217

talia's guide to weeknight drinking

For many reasons, I'm lucky to have Talia Baiocchi, editor in chief of *PUNCH,* a cool online magazine about cocktail and drink culture, in my life. For your wine and *aperitivo* purposes, read on! Her weeknight drinking guide will have you spritzing it up and navigating wine shelves in no time.

EASY-DRINKING APERITIVI

Do as the Italians: Before you even reach for the pot or pasta, start your evening off with an *aperitivo* cocktail. In Italy, this is typically referred to as a spritz—a low-alcohol, bitter, bubbly cocktail that is simple to make, forgiving, and begs to be riffed on. Below is a collection of classic and modern *aperitivi,* from the frothy Garibaldi to a summer spritz we love to whip up on a whim.

VENETIAN SPRITZ

MAKES 1 COCKTAIL

The standard bearer of #spritzlife throughout Italy, the classic formula can be made with a range of bitter liqueurs, but is most commonly served with Aperol.

2 ounces bitter liqueur (such as Aperol, Campari, Contratto Bitter, or Cappelletti Aperitivo Americano)
3 to 4 ounces Prosecco
2 ounces soda water
Orange slice and olive, for garnish

To a rocks or wine glass filled with ice, add the liqueur, Prosecco, then the soda water. Top with the garnish and serve.

NEGRONI SBAGLIATO

MAKES 1 COCKTAIL

The Negroni's bubbly, lower-proof sister, the Negroni Sbagliato—whose addendum translates to "mistaken" or "incorrect"—was supposedly created by accident at Milan's Basso in the 1970s, when barman Mirko Stocchetto reached for a bottle of Prosecco in place of gin.

1 ounce Campari
1 ounce sweet vermouth
3 ounces Prosecco
Orange slice, for garnish

To a rocks or wine glass filled with ice, add the Campari, sweet vermouth, then the Prosecco. Top with the garnish and serve.

GARIBALDI

MAKES 1 COCKTAIL

The Garibaldi is traditionally just equal parts Campari and fresh orange juice. But this version dials back the Campari ratio a bit (in a nod to Naren Young's excellent version at Dante in New York) and tops it with Prosecco.

1½ ounces Campari

3½ ounces fresh orange juice

Prosecco, for topping off

Orange slice, for garnish

To a Collins glass filled with ice, add the Campari and orange juice. Stir to combine, then top with the Prosecco and garnish.

HUDSON SUMMER SPRITZ

MAKES 1 COCKTAIL

This simple combo of summer greenmarket bounty and, well, booze became my summer 2015 staple.

½ ounce Giffard crème de Pamplemousse Rose

2 leaves basil, torn into pieces, plus an extra sprig for garnish

1 ounce watermelon juice

1½ ounces Campari

Prosecco, for topping off

Sprig of basil, for garnish

In a rocks glass, gently muddle the Pamplemousse and basil. Add some ice and the watermelon juice and Campari. Stir to combine and top with the Prosecco and the basil sprig.

WINTER SPRITZ

MAKES 1 COCKTAIL

While the spritz is most associated with outdoor drinking, with a swap of in-season citrus it can easily transition to fall or winter.

½ ounce Amaro Braulio

1 ounce Cappelletti Aperitivo Americano

1 ounce blood orange juice

Prosecco, for topping off

Blood orange slice, for garnish

To a Collins glass filled with ice, add the Amaro Braulio, Cappellitti Aperitivo Americano, and blood orange juice. Top with Prosecco and the blood orange slice and serve.

BACK POCKET WINE

What you want from a back pocket wine is both affordability (under $25, in this case) and sessionability—that is, you should be able to drink half the bottle right quick. (Think juicy, high-acid reds from Beaujolais, or the mineral, sneakily complex whites of Muscadet.) But a lower price point doesn't mean it needs to taste like the bland Pinot Grigio you get at the airport. Quite the opposite: A great back pocket wine should punch above its weight class, and offer complexity and intrigue. Here's where to look:

BEAUJOLAIS

While the best wines from Beaujolais have steadily risen in price over the last decade (and rightfully so), this is still one of the world's great wine regions for value, particularly if you're in the market for juicy, mineral high-acid reds (you are).

Look for: Domaine des Terres Dorees (Jean-Paul Brun), Michel Guignier, Clos de la Roilette, Julien Sunier
Pair with: Radiatore with Potatoes, Kale & Bacon; Proposal Pasta with Roasted Chicken & Mushrooms; Rigatoni alla Norma

SICILY

Sicily is a big island that produces a heck of a lot of wine, but if you know where to look, it's a veritable treasure chest of bright, easy-drinking reds. Look to Vittoria in the southeastern end of the island, where you'll find vibrant, happy reds—made from Frappato and Nero d'Avola, often blended together in the Cerasuolo di Vittoria appellation—that are still complex enough to warrant contemplation. Many of the whites, made

primarily from Grillo or Carricante grapes, are worth seeking out as well.

Look for: Arianna Occhipinti, Tami, COS, Valle dell'Acate, Gulfi
Pair with: Pasta Puttanesca; Creamy Saffron Risotto-Style Fregola; Strozzapreti with Broccolini, Anchovy & Almonds; Moroccan Lamb Ragu

CAMPANIA

In the eyes of most consumers, Campania makes its bones on Aglianico, the region's primary red grape and the source of tannic, brooding wines that channel their volcanic roots. But there's a gentler side to the region, primarily if you're on the hunt for whites. From the smoky, rich Fiano to lean and mineral Greco di Tufo to the light touch and florality of Falanghina, the region's coastal whites are a world unto themselves—and one best explored with a plateful of seafood pasta.

Look for: Pietracupa, Ciro Picariello, Bellus, Mastroberardino, De Conciliis, Luigi Maffini
Pair with: Pasta with Summer Squash, Sardines & Preserved Lemon; Baccalà & Green Olive Pasta with Almonds; Spaghetti alla Foriana; Rotini with Rainbow Chard & Orange Fennel Ricotta

THE ALPS

The Alps aren't all après-ski, fondue, and Julie Andrews—they're also home to a cluster of world-class wine regions, notably Italy's Valle d'Aosta and Trentino-Alto Adige and France's Savoie. These regions share two things in common: high-acid whites (look for Petite Arvine in Valle d'Aosta, Altesse in Savoie and Weissburgunder [Pinot Blanc] from Alto Adige) and spicy reds of varying weights. On the red side, a lighter touch can be found in Fumin, Cornalin, and even Gamay in Valle d'Aosta, and Marzemino and Schiava in Trentino-Alto Adige. For a bit more junk in the trunk without losing that alpine freshness, look for Mondeuse in Savoie and Teroldego in Trentino-Alto Adige.

Look for: Savoie—Franck Peillot, Jacques Maillet, Domaine Belluard; Valle d'Aosta: Diego Curtaz, Grosjean Frères, Ermes Pavese; Trentino-Alto Adige: Foradori, Vallarom, Weingut Niklas, Abbazia di Novacella
Pair with: Penne Rigate with Gorgonzola, Radicchio & Walnuts; Buttery Basil Pesto with Linguine

PIEDMONT

When it comes to wine, Piedmont isn't exactly the first place one might think to look for a weeknight wine. This is the land of Barolo and Barbaresco—the crowned king and queen of Italian wine, with the price tags to prove it. But it's also a region of staggering diversity and a grab bag of more lesser-known wines that are born pasta BFFs. On the light side, look to peppery Pelaverga and juicy Grignolino, high-acid Barbera, and plush, fruity Dolcetto. And if you need something that can go toe-to-toe with richer pastas, Freisa is your friend.

Look for: G.B. Burlotto, Castello di Verduno, G.D. Vajra, Giuseppe Mascarello & Figlio, Crivelli
Pair with: Paparadelle with Duck Confit, Olives & Raisins; Two-Step Tortellini en Brodo; Easter Ham Carbonara

JEREZ

Every proper stock of weeknight pasta wines needs at least one dark horse. Or two. Fino and Manzanilla sherries have made a break from the tapas bar in recent years. Salty, bone dry, and served with a healthy chill, this style of sherry is a shoo-in with vegetable-based dishes (even those containing wine's mortal enemies, artichokes and asparagus) and seafood.

Look for: Valdespino, La Guita, Gutiérrez Colosía, Fernando de Castilla, El Maestro Sierra
Pair with: Fideos with Cockles & Chorizo; Pasta with Mussels & Pecornio; Caramelized Fennel & Hazelnut Pasta; Linguine with Asparagus & Lemon; Scallops, Sun Golds & a Mess of Herbs

NEW CALIFORNIA AND OREGON

No longer the primary domain of white linen and over-oaked Chardonnay, the "New California" (so-called by our friend who literally wrote the book on it, Jon Bonné) is a place where you can now drink better for cheaper. And it won't just be Cabernet and Chardonnay: The new kids on the block (alongside steadfast pioneers) are playing with new grapes and new growing regions.

The same is true for Oregon. Exceptional and affordable, Gamay, Riesling, Cabernet Franc, and more now hold court alongside some of the best Pinot to be found in America.

Look for: California—Broc Cellars, Lieu Dit, Jolie-Laide, Matthiasson (and their second label, Tendu), Ryme Cellars; Oregon: Bow & Arrow, Teutonic Wine Company, Montinore Estate, Division Winemaking Company
Pair with: "BLT" Pasta; Pasta with Leeks; Poblano Chile Risotto

stocking up

The true beauty of back pocket pasta is that it prevents that last-minute dash to the supermarket on the way home from work. But any improvised cooking is only as good as a cook's pantry. So for the most versatility, stock up on flavorful essentials that have some shelf life, then fill in the gaps with fresh produce and herbs. You may not want to go out and buy all of these ingredients at once. Start with the basics that you're familiar with (olive oil, garlic, Pecorino Romano, lemons), then slowly add an ingredient or two (capers, nuts, anchovy paste) to keep you interested and inspired.

IN THE PANTRY

OLIVE OIL: When I can get to Arthur Avenue in the Bronx, I stock up on unfiltered, grassy Sicilian olive oil, which I pick up at Teitel Brothers. But California Olive Ranch and Lucini are frequently found stoveside in my kitchen. I cook with extra-virgin, which is the highest quality (recommended when cooking with so few ingredients). It should taste fruity, spicy, and a little bitter in flavor.

GARLIC: I keep two to three heads around, just in case. They make an appearance in most of my recipes. Sometimes you want garlic bread, too!

CAPERS: Briny and pungent, capers add great flavor to any dish. I buy mine packed in salt. Make sure to rinse them well (let them hang out in a bowl of water, sometimes changing the water once) before using to ensure you don't end up with a salt bomb.

NUTS: I'm never without a large variety, including almonds, hazelnuts, pine nuts, pistachios, and walnuts. They offer great crunch and healthy fats and make a good addition to most pastas. They're versatile, too, equally good raw or toasted and tossed in salads.

CANNED SAN MARZANO TOMATOES: Without fail, I have four 28-ounce cans on hand at all times. In my opinion, they are the best tomatoes for making sauce. Stick to cans of whole tomatoes, which you can crush by hand, or diced if you're feeling lazy; avoid crushed, which I find too thick for most sauces.

CRUSHED RED PEPPER FLAKES: Buy these organic and keep them within reach by the salt and pepper. I also love *chile de árbol* and Aleppo—the latter is a Syrian pepper, which has a smokier flavor.

BREADCRUMBS: I prefer panko breadcrumbs because they last forever in the pantry. I never buy the seasoned kind. Stick to plain toast and flavor on your own with citrus, garlic, and fresh herbs.

WHITE VERMOUTH: I always keep this around for deglazing dishes. Water and broth work, too, but the white vermouth adds a gentle herbaceous quality and keeps forever. It's also great in martinis!

CHICKEN STOCK: If you make your own, good for you! I do frequently and freeze it. But I also keep a few boxes of stock tucked away for quick use.

FLAKY SALT: I use the brands Maldon or Jacobsen as a garnish for everything that I cook, and I also put it out on the table for people to use if they wish. I love the way the large crystals look, and the flavor and crunch cannot be beat.

KOSHER SALT: I find kosher salt best for seasoning, and I use it to salt my pasta water. I prefer Diamond Crystal or Morton's.

TINNED FISH: I like having a variety of tinned fish in my pantry, as they can be easily turned into a healthy, protein-packed meal. I keep Italian tuna packed in oil, sardines, anchovies, and clams. If I know ahead of time that I want to make linguine with clams, I'll buy them fresh, but canned work fine on the fly.

WHITE BEANS: Beans are a good staple to pull together a quick, hearty pasta. Progesso, Goya, and Eden Organics are all great brands. If you have the time to cook your own from scratch, please do! Rancho Gordo and Bob's Red Mill are my favorite brands.

IN THE FRIDGE

ONIONS, CARROTS, AND CELERY: There's little you can't do if these three vegetables are in your crisper. Cook onion, carrots, and celery together and you have *soffrito*, which is a great base for meaty ragus and other sauces. I keep an assortment of onions such as red, yellow, shallots, and leeks and use them interchangeably.

HERBS: I buy all of them, all the time! I'm a big believer in having lots in the fridge. Adding in fresh herbs before plating a meal gives it brightness, extra flavor, and beautiful color. Flat-leaf Italian parsley is high on my list, as well as basil, chives, mint, oregano, rosemary, tarragon, thyme, and sage.

FRESH CHILES: I love heat, and in the summer I buy fresh chiles wherever I can find them. Cayennes and serranos are my favorites.

LEAFY GREENS: Sometimes I put arugula on top of pasta because I'm too tired to make a salad. You can also toss greens in at the end before plating to get a good wilt. I recommend arugula, escarole, pea shoots, spinach, mustard greens, and lacinato kale.

ANCHOVY PASTE: While I use tinned anchovies frequently, I find these tubes convenient to use as they last forever in the fridge. This paste is great in salad dressings as well. Anchovy paste is stronger than straightforward fillets, so I tend to use less rather than more. You can always add in additional amounts later.

DOUBLE-CONCENTRATED TOMATO PASTE: A tablespoon or two adds richness to tomato-based sauces. I prefer the kind in a tube that I can keep in the fridge, and I like the Amore brand.

CHEESES:

• **Hard and salty:** All three of these cheeses are wonderful grated over pasta. They have distinct yet understated differences and are imported from different parts of Italy. They are beautiful on their own, but also can be mixed together.

• **Grana Padano PDO:** A sweet, hard cow's milk cheese made in the Po River Valley of northern Italy, this is made with skimmed milk and has a subtle and less salty flavor than Parmigiano-Reggiano, to which it is often compared. It also tends to be less expensive than Parmesan and has a pleasant, granular texture. It should be aged for at least twelve months, but no more than thirty. The younger cheese is softer and better for grating into pasta. The aged cheese makes a good pre-dinner snack.

• **Parmesan (Parmigiano-Reggiano):** This cheese is primarily named after the provinces in which it is made, Parma and Reggio Emilia. It is a hard cow's milk cheese, but is aged longer that Grana Padano and can be nuttier in flavor and grittier in texture.

• **Pecorino Romano:** The saltiest and sharpest cheese of the bunch, this is one of the oldest cheeses in Italy. It's also my personal workhorse. Made with 100 percent sheep's milk, it ages anywhere from eight to twelve months. When younger, it has a softer texture and sweeter taste. (I prefer it aged.)

SOFT AND CREAMY DAIRY: Stir your favorites into pasta when it's finished for richness, or place a dollop on top of a meat sauce to add creaminess. Listed in order of mild to tangy: ricotta, Greek yogurt, labneh, and crème fraîche.

EGGS: Buy the freshest you can find. If you can buy them directly from a farm or farmers' market, I encourage it. If they are store-bought, I recommend large, brown, and organic.

BACON OR PANCETTA: These two items can easily be interchanged, depending on which is easier to find or whatever you happen to have on hand. Bacon will impart a smokier flavor than pancetta, and if you do use it, I prefer slab-cut because it gives you the ability to control the thickness of your dice.

CITRUS: My fridge is always stocked full of lemons (Meyer ones when they are in season), oranges, limes, grapefruits—you name it. I zest them for stirring into breadcrumbs or squeeze them over a dish to add acidity and brightness.

BUTTER: I recommend using only unsalted for cooking. You'll be salting as you cook and can better control the amount.

recipe index

acknowledgments

First and foremost, I have the deepest gratitude for my editor, Angelin Borsics, who was patient, kind, and gently guided me through this process. You've made me a better writer, and your support and friendship means the world.

To Clarkson Potter associate publisher Doris Cooper, I fiercely love you. Thank you for your unwavering belief in me and in *Back Pocket Pasta*.

To all my ladies at Clarkson Potter, I adore you, and you are nothing short of amazing. I'm looking at you Amanda Englander, Kate Tyler, Rica Allannic, Anna Mintz, Carly Gorga, and Stephanie Huntwork.

To Clarkson Potter publisher Aaron Wehner. Thank you for listening. I cold pitched you a book idea after a few glasses of wine and you empowered me to write it. I am grateful.

To my agent, Kim Witherspoon, for believing in me and in this project. I also cold pitched you that same night! Stars aligned.

Deepest, humblest, tearing up thinking about it, thanks to my creative team. To my photographers, Peden + Munk (Taylor and Jen), you are brilliant and I am your biggest fan. Thank you for trusting in this project when it was a seedling of an idea and seeing it through from proposal to published book. You guys are so *molto buono* it hurts. To my food stylists, Rebecca Jurkevich and Sue Li, and prop stylists, Amy Wilson and Nina Lalli, for making pasta look and feel like there is no reason for any other food ever. I am so honored that you all took on this book with me. Your talents are immeasurable.

Sweet Jenny Beal Davis, thank you for your work on this beautifully designed book. I've known you long before I started in this industry and there was no question on who would work on this with me.

To Talia Baiocchi for being the best friend a girl could ask for. Thank you for lending your voice to this project, and for being a constant source of inspiration and guidance. I love you so much.

To Andrew Arrick and Michael Hofemann and Michael and Caroline Ventura for allowing me to play house in your homes. I am forever grateful. I'm not sure how, but I'll get you back one day, I promise.

To Laura Arnold, my recipe tester, thank you for making pasta so many, many times.

To my darling friend Marnie Hanel for telling me to write this book. You make me feel invincible.

To my incredible friends for your help, loyalty, and inspiration in so many different ways: answering frantic questions, brainstorming ideas, recipe testing, cheering me on when I most needed it, and leaving me alone when I needed that, too. That's you, Tamar Adler; Nils Bernstein; Seth Bodie; Pablo Douzoglou and Amanda Kludt; Gabrielle Gulielmetti and Rachel Sanzone; Jasmine Hirsch; Jon, Leslie, and Eli Feldman; Eva Karagiorgas; Andrew Mariani and Lia Ices; Jenn McCormick and Steve Panawek; Carissa Mondavi; Carla Lalli Music; Laura Neilson; Katie Parla; Suzy Pasette; Doria Santlofer; Ashley Santoro; Anthony Sasso; Sarah and Nick Suarez; Kevin Tienhaara and Tommy Champine; Julia Turshen; Eliot Kessel and Jersey Walz; and Kevin Walz.

To Desiree Gruber for believing in me from the get-go and telling me I could do whatever it was that I wanted, I just needed to figure out what it was. And to Kyle MacLachlan for being so very supportive and for being the most fun sing-along partner.

Also, thank you to the gals at BeccaPR, Rochelle Billow, Meredith Bradford, Tony Biancosino, Chloe Mata Crane, Melania Dunea, Annabelle Dunne, Marie La France, Laura Ferrara, Andrew Keegan, Kristin Marchesi, Christine Muhlke, Leslie Pariseau, Ray Pirkle and everyone at Rivertown Lodge, Jodi Rappaport, Nikki Reiss, Alison Roman, Lily Soysal, Andrea Strong, Melissa Poll, and Team Ischia.

To all of the Goodmans, I love you. Uncle Michael, thank you for keeping Nonni's stories alive, and to Aunt Philippa for digging through files and sending me old recipes that I asked for frequently and urgently, and to cousin Jonathan for your contribution.

To my sissy, Cara Henry-Schiller, I love you beyond words.

To my parents, Brian and Mia Henry, for encouraging me to be the creative spirit that I am and for believing that I could do anything if I set my mind to it. I love you both deeply.

And finally, to the guy who matters most, my husband, Chad Silver. Thank you a million times for everything you have done and for helping me "paint my way out of the corner." This book wouldn't have happened without you. I love you from the bottom of my heart.

index

·NOTE: PAGE REFERENCES IN *ITALICS* INDICATE PHOTOGRAPHS.